A Guest in Azerbaijan

Barbara Lutterbeck

A Guest in Azerbaijan

with texts by Brunhild Seeler-Herzog

Culture & Cuisine

WIENAND

Contents

Foreword

The "Land of Fire" harbours a vast hoard of beautiful features and treasures. Culture, art, and sports as well as a wide range of tourist attractions in general make a journey to Azerbaijan a worthwhile undertaking.

The capital, Baku, the "City of Winds", looks vast; the modern architecture stands alongside immaculately maintained buildings from the turn of the last century dating from the time of the first oil boom at the end of the nineteenth and beginning of the twentieth century. Its metropolitain flair with bustling traffic and smart international shops contrasts harmoniously with the comparatively small walled Old City and the historic city gates, which have been included on the UNESCO World Cultural Heritage list since 2000. Here you can stroll through the narrow alleys where merchants hawk their goods as they have done since time immemorial.

As a result of my profession, my perception tends to be a visual and sensory one, and so, despite the contrasts, I sensed a harmony between history and modernity. I was impressed by the city's appearance, shaped by the interplay between the sandstone-coloured city palazzi and the mirrored façades of the skyscrapers . They appear again on the surface of the waters of the Caspian Sea in atmospheric reflections in the warm light of the evening sun.

The Azerbaijanis themselves struck me as being equally harmonious. They are a friendly people with a remarkable number of very attractive women. Their strong sense of family and love of children are evident on walks through the city and when strolling along the promenade. With regard to their hospitality towards strangers, they also live up in all respects to the reputation of Azerbaijan.

No less memorable were my lasting impressions of the profound beauty of the interior of the country. Azerbaijan invites visitors to go hiking, skiing or – like me – to take photographs. Extensive regions are almost empty of human settlement, which underlines the grandeur of the natural surroundings. I travelled to Azerbaijan in mid-August, and the harvest season which was just over rewarded us with a cornucopia of fruits, a happy coincidence with regard to the chapter of this book devoted to the cuisine of Azerbaijan. Azerbaijan is a rich country in the true sense of the word – rich not only in natural resources but also in nature and culture.

Unfortunately I was not able to visit some of the wonderful and unique regions of the country, including Nagorno-Karabakh, historically an integral part of Azerbaijan, because the region and seven surrounding districts are occupied by Armenia. It is still my sincere wish to visit this ancient cradle of culture and art, which is also known as the "Conservatoire of the Caucasus" and which is the home of many famous artists, including Uzeyir Hajibeyli, Khurshidbanu Natavan (1832–1897) and others. I sincerely hope that a solution to the conflict will be found so that peace can return to Nagorno-Karabakh.

Barbara Lutterbeck

The Country Azerbaijan

In the rocks of Gobustan, today part of the UNESCO World Cultural Heritage, rock paintings and petroglyphs depicting male and female figures, various wild animals, hunting scenes, ritual dances, and sacrifices reveal that the history of the settlement of Azerbaijan extends back over several thousand years. The country forms the largest part of the southern Caucasus region and lies to the west of Asia Minor, east of the Caspian Sea and adjacent to and south of Iran. Authors of Antiquity including for example Herodotus, Ptolemy, Aristotle, and especially Strabo in his *Geographica* desribed the region as a melting pot of cultures and languages. In Roman times, 130 interpreters ensured that, in spite of the 300-odd languages spoken in the Caucasus region, trade could flourish and corresponding agreements were concluded. Azerbaijan lay at the strategically important intersection between various empires, changing allegiances at various times – for example to the Persian, Arabian, Russian, and Mongolian empires. Accordingly, dependencies and wars were inevitable and continued until recent times. The result during the early nineteenth century was that the traditional regions settled by the Azerbaijanis were split into two. Historic North Azerbaijan was known as "Albania" until the arrival of Islam (but should not be confused, however, with the country of Albania in the Balkans) and thereafter as "Arran". It consisted not only of the region occupied today by the Republic of Azerbaijan with its population of about 9.7 million inhabitants but also included the north-western province of the Islamic Republic of Iran, which bears the same name, and which has a population of more than 40 million inhabitants.

The people continue to be united by their common language. The South Azerbaijani language, a Turkic language related to Turkish, is spoken by some 50 million people worldwide. Moreover, they are also linked by their faith, which is Islam. The Islam practised in the Republic of Azerbaijan is a moderate form. Adherents of other faiths are treated with tolerance and visitors are encountered with great friendliness and hospitality. As early as 1375, Abraham Cresques, Mallorca's "Master of World Maps and Compasses", included cities like Baku and Shamakhi in his Portolan map, the famous "Catalan Atlas". In doing so, he took up the reports of the Venetian explorer Marco Polo, who some 100 years previously had written enthusiastically of the "golden and silver silk fabrics" of Shamakhi and who had been amazed in Baku at the large quantities of oil, which was "aromatic and cured camel mange". Arabian travellers also wrote reports of the "green, black and white oil, as white as jasmine".

We know from records dating back to the sixth century BC that mineral oil has played a role for the economy of Azerbaijan for the past 2,700 years and that it was used for medical and military purposes as well as for heating and oil lamps. Initially it was collected in shallow pits, from which it was siphoned off; in the sixteenth century these shafts, which were dug out by hand, already reached depths of 35 metres; by 1886 the oil drillings reached depths of 50 to 315 metres. A regular boom began from the second half of the nineteenth century. In 1898, with the help of foreign capital and business tycoons like the Nobels and the Rothschilds, whose spectacular city palaces can still be admired in Baku today, the output of oil in Baku exceeded that of America. In fact, it had become the world's biggest petroleum drilling region. At the end of the nineteenth century, oil tankers were introduced, and between 1897 and 1907 what in those days was the world's longest pipeline – made of Mannesmann pipes – linked Baku with Batumi on the Black Sea, over 800 kilometres away. In the mid-twentieth century, offshore oil drilling also began in Azerbaijan, and in 1994 eleven major oil firms from seven countries signed the so-called "Contract of the Century", an agreement regarding the joint exploitation of several oil fields in the Azerbaijani section of the Caspian Sea. In the meantime, 30 corporations and 20 countries with 32 contracts have also adopted this agreement.

The vast Shah Deniz gas field lies at a depth of 500 metres beneath the waters of the Caspian Sea, some 70 kilometres southeast of Baku; its gas stocks amount to more than 1.2 trillion cubic metres. The petroleum and natural gas stocks in the Caspian Sea are said to be the third-largest in the world. In the north of the Apsheron Peninsula you can almost forget the oil drills, however. The Caspian Sea covers an area of 386,400 square kilometres and is almost 1,000 metres deep in places; it is about 650 times the size of Lake Constance.

The waters of the Caspian Sea harbour a treasure of a very different kind: the sturgeon with its valuable caviar. In 2014, however, a ban on sturgeon fishing was agreed for the following five years in order to encourage the recovery of stocks. Nonetheless, other fish, including the Caspian kutum (Caspian whitefish) and carp are carefully prepared, either grilled or stuffed with the walnuts which are frequently used in large quantities in many dishes, and then baked in the oven. The basic rule of the excellent local cuisine is that the best and freshest ingredients of the season are used, either from the market or from one's own garden. The specialities taste particularly good with a glass of wine. Azerbaijan's wine and spirits production can be traced back to settlers from southern Germany, who arrived here between 1816 and 1819. Over the following years they founded the wine-growing villages of Helenendorf (Khanlar) and Annenfeld (Shamkir) near Ganja. Some 40 percent of the population still works in agriculture to this day.

In stark contrast to the Caspian Sea, which lies 28 metres below sea level, stands Azerbaijan's Mount Bazardyuzi in the Caucasus, which is 4,466 metres high. This mountain once represented the end of the world. It was regarded as the rock to which Prometheus was chained because he had brought the divine fire down to Earth for mankind, and where he was compelled to endure torture for centuries, until he was freed by Hercules. In Azerbaijan fire was regarded as being especially divine above all because for centuries it has even flared up directly out of the earth. The fire-worshippers paid homage in their Zoroastrian temples to its purifying effects. Today the three futuristic Flame Towers in the capital Baku symbolise Azerbaijan, the modern "Land of Fire".

The City Baku

THE METROPOLIS ON THE CASPIAN SEA

The metropolitan flair is evident as the plane comes in to land: the capital of Azerbaijan welcomes visitors with an imposing skyline, whose ultra-modern buildings seem to rise directly out of the Caspian Sea. The country's wealth lies in this, the world's largest lake, and its gas and oil fields. As a result, the port is the most important economic centre and also the hub of many oil pipelines. In August 1918, when Britain marched into Baku with a troop of 1,000 soldiers, the English newspaper Near East wrote that the oil from Baku was unrivalled. "If oil is the queen, then Baku is her throne", observed Winston Churchill, and that rapidly becomes clear as you immerse yourself in this remarkable and exciting city. Although uncrowned, the oil magnates planned their private residences and corporate headquarters in magnificent style. In many cases these city palaces, mostly built of sandstone in around 1900, were designed as copies to scale of European models. They gleam in shades of ochre in a wide variety of styles. Many of them are eclectic in design, like the majestic Palace of Hajinskiy, in which General de Gaulle spent the night in 1944 on his way to Moscow.

Not far away stands the defiant, unadorned Maiden Tower, dating from the twelfth century. It was built at a time when people were just beginning to build art-historically important structures of Islamic culture. These included the Palace of the Shirvanshahs as well as hammams and mosques in what is now the Old City, today part of the UNESCO World Cultural Heritage. Here narrow medieval alleys radiate their charm while the new Baku greets visitors with broad avenues, manicured squares, and expansive parks. Mediterranean flair dominates on the lively lakeside promenade fringed with cafés, restaurants, and shopping malls. Especially in the warm summer months it is a bustling and popular avenue for strolling along. The opera house, which also stages ballets, is indicative of prosperity and an active cultural life, as is the concert hall. There are several stages for jazz und *mugham* as well as various theatres and museums. The city acts as host to international forums and events in politics, science, and culture, including the annual international Mstislav Rostropovich Festival, the Global Baku Forum, and the World Forum of Intercultural Dialogue. In 2012 Baku hosted the Eurovision Song Contest and the first European Games were held here in 2015. Baku is also the well-connected seat of several universities and research institutes.

One of the cradles of human settlement, Baku is at the cutting edge as regards architecture. The Heydar Aliyev Centre, for example, is a futuristic structure in immaculate white and without a single straight line; it is an approach to the "eternal skies", a link between past, present, and even future. Baku's landmark is the three reflecting Flame Towers, whose lambent "flames" rise heavenwards, proudly symbolising the "Land of Fire" – because that is precisely the meaning of the word "Azerbaijan".

THE OLD CITY

Compared with the pulsating City with its roaring traffic, the Old City is almost an oasis of calm. It is partly hidden away behind the massive walled fortifications and has been included on the UNESCO World Cultural Heritage list since 2000. Cars are largely banned here and so visitors can simply allow themselves to be carried along, browsing round the little shops and craftsmen's workshops and strolling through the alleys paved with rough cobblestones. Some alleys are so narrow that the imaginatively designed wooden balconies and oriel windows jutting out from the houses seem almost to touch the house wall on the opposite side. Here and there, a landing may be in use as a display for carpets, or elsewhere for a game of backgammon; and in between, tea rooms and hammams wait for customers.

The hammam of the famous Palace of the Shirvanshahs also had at its disposal an extensive system for the various bathing procedures. This complex was built in the middle of the fifteenth century and extended on a number of occasions. It was only rediscovered in 1939. It was partly constructed underground to keep it warm in winter and cool in summer. It also includes the elaborately decorated mausoleum of the rulers and the oldest building in the complex, perched on the summit of a hill: a two-storey residence begun in 1411 with 52 rooms and the Divankhana, or courthouse. The latter is an architectural jewel in the form of an octagonal rotunda with a domed roof and arcades with Gothic arches; its ornate decoration, filigree ornamentations symbolising figs and vine leaves, allows us to speculate that official receptions and court hearings took place here. The Shah's mosque is small and fairly sober, but has a notable moulding around the 22-metre-high minaret. Among the well-preserved or restored structures in the Old City are also the Mohammed Mosque, constructed in 1078 of hewn stones, and the unadorned Siniggala Minaret, as well as the world-famous caravanserais, which today frequently serve as restaurants. In the separate niches, which were once the sleeping quarters and stables within their 500-year-old walls, you can savour the specialities of Azerbaijani cuisine, sometimes even to the sounds of *mugham* music.

Baku's main landmark, the Maiden Tower, dates from the twelfth century or possibly even earlier. It is 28 metres high and impossible to overlook. The view from its platform encompasses simultaneously all the styles of architecture in the city: the buildings of the Old City, the city palaces of the oil magnates from the turn of the last century, the impressive corporate headquarters and the high-rise buildings from the Soviet era, together with the large-scale futuristic structures of the present and finally the source of the city's wealth: the Caspian Sea.

THE MUKHTAROV HOUSE

In the thirteenth century, Marco Polo was amazed to discover that on the Absheron Peninsula the oil flowed so fast that it was possible to load up more than 100 camels at once so that they could transport it via the Silk Road in leather sacks. Some 600 years later, not only entrepreneurs like the Nobels and the Rothschilds took advantage of the opportunities provided by the petroleum boom that was just getting under way; numerous Azerbaijanis also became important oil magnates through a combination of daring and business acumen. They included Haji Zeynalabdin Taghiyev, Ağa Shamsi Asadullayev and Ağa Murtusa Mukhtarov, a man of modest origins who became an oil millionaire. He had his Polish architect Józef Ploszko build a palace in Baku in the French Gothic style. After it was finished, he led his wife into the magnificent residence and surprised her by announcing: "This is your house; you are its mistress." When the Red Army invaded in 1920, he announced that no Red Army soldier would ever step inside his house in army boots. When, however, two soldiers even rode their horses through the rooms, Mukhtarov shot first them and then himself. His wife was able to escape and survived into the 1950s. Since the palace had been built for love, it serves today as the "Palace of Happiness" where marriages are registered.

THE HEYDAR ALIYEV MONUMENT

Today, the Republic of Azerbaijan is ruled as a sovereign nation state by the president, Ilham Aliyev, whose aim is to achieve a closer relationship with the European Community. His father, Heydar Aliyev (1923–2003), was the third president of the young republic, which became independent after the collapse of the Soviet Union. He made a considerable mark on the country during his period in office from 1993 until his death in 2003. He is highly respected as the "Architect of modern Azerbaijan", since he had a decisive influence on the rebuilding and growth of the country and its development and stability, as well as the local culture and its maintenance. Furthermore, a large number of important international agreements were reached on his initiative. A contract was signed with Western oil companies in 1994 during his rule concerning the exploitation of oil fields in the Caspian Sea. It included the construction of an own pipeline and has entered the annals of history as a "contract of the century".

Aliyev began to implement important reforms in order to align the country gradually with international standards in both its foreign and domestic policy. Today many institutions also continue Heydar Aliyev's ideas at international level, including, for example, the Heydar Aliyev Foundation. It is directed by the First Lady of Azerbaijan, Mehriban Aliyeva, and is responsible amongst other things for the education of young Azerbaijanis, the promotion of artists, and the staging of worldwide cultural events. The Heydar Aliyev Centre is a cultural and educational institution with numerous exhibitions and concerts from classic to modern. The spectacular building was designed by the British-Iraqi star architect Zaha Hadid and it underlines the ambition of the city of Baku to create a stir on the architectural scene.

The Heydar Aliyev Monument by Omar Eldarov is visited frequently, not only only during the Flower Festival, which is held there annually.

THE VEILED WOMAN

On 28 May 1918, the Democratic Republic of Azerbaijan was proclaimed in Tiflis, the capital of Georgia. This state was the first parliamentary democracy in the Islamic world and it existed for just 23 months. In 1920 the Soviet Russians occupied the country and annexed it politically as the Azerbaijani Socialist Soviet Republic. In its short existence, however, the Democratic Republic achieved important political progress, including the right to vote for women, which was introduced at that time.

A number of remarkable stages in the history of Azerbaijani women followed: thus they were the first women in the East to abandon the veil. The Soviet era opened up a number of professional opportunities for them: as artists, politicians, and scientists or military careers, for example as pilots. Leyla Mammadbeyova, for example, was the first female pilot not only in Azerbaijan and the Caucasus, but also in Southern Europe and the Middle East. The self-awareness of Azerbaijani women has its roots in the country's oriental tradition, which they continue to cultivate, but they have also been influenced by the Soviet worldview and nowadays they are strongly oriented towards Western Europe. Furthermore, the upheavals in Eastern Europe have also contributed to turning Azerbaijani women into modern, emancipated women, who also face up to the demands and challenges of the present day and who take an active part in politics. There is a State Committee for Family, Women, and Children's Affairs, and open discussions are held in the media on female-specific topics and issues.

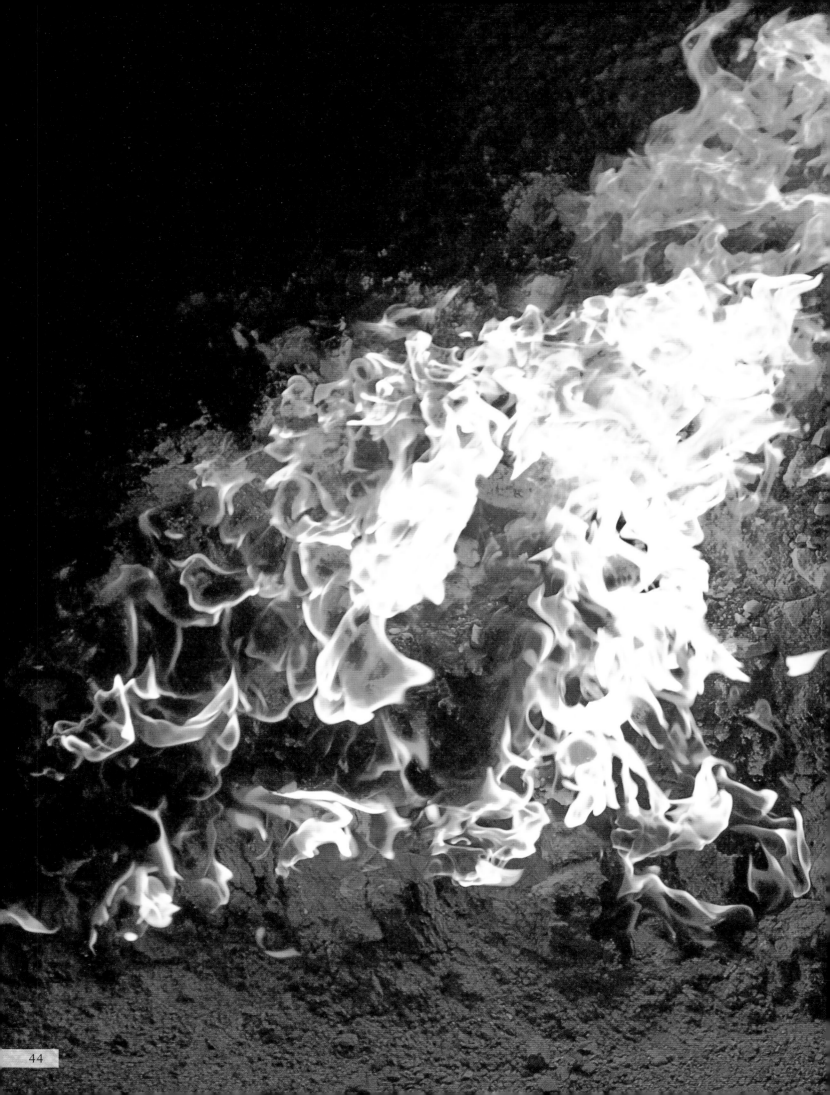

YANAR DAG

On Yanar Dag, the "Burning Mountain", a few kilometres north of Baku, metre-high flames shoot directly out of the earth – a fascinating spectacle, especially after dark. Like the country's spectacular mud volcanoes, they are fed by natural gas which gathers above a bubble of oil. Back in the thirteenth century, Marco Polo had reported in amazement that there were vast amounts of combustible oil on the Absheron Peninsula.

A tea room and a picnic site can be found on a slope above the fire pit. Groups of young people and families with children gather here to enjoy the atmosphere.

A MODERN CITY
IN THE ORIENT

"He who knows himself and others
Here will also see,
That the East and West, like brothers,
Parted ne'er shall be."
 (Johann Wolfgang von Goethe)

These words from Goethe's *West-Eastern Divan* are
particularly relevant in Azerbaijan. Indeed, in Baku
the Orient and the Occident are now impossible to
separate and the boundaries between East and West
are fluid. Islam here has a spiritual aura, and tolerance
is practised towards other religions. Here it is possible
to move without difficulty between both worlds, cul-
turally, emotionally, and architecturally, in the contrast
between futuristic architecture and Oriental-Islamic
buildings.

THE BLUE MOSQUE OF BAKU

This mosque, perched on a hill, owes its name to the intense blue of its dome: Göy Mescid, Blue Mosque. Its other name is Ittifaq-Union, because with this building, erected between 1912 and 1913, Haji Ejdar Bey Ashurbeyov aimed to create a joint place of prayer for both Sunnis and Shias. The architect Ziver Bey Ahmadbeyov developed the project for this elegant and spacious house of prayer, which together with the Taza Pir Mosque also remained open for the faithful during the Soviet Era.

HAMMAM

There used to be a hammam in every district of the city, and the weekly visit to the steam bath served not only for personal care purposes but also to maintain personal contacts, up to and including arranged marriages for sons or daughters. National Art Museum of Azerbaijan shows many of the utensils which people took with them to the baths – small decorated copper caskets, for example, in which women would lock up their jewellery and hand it to the female pool attendant. The picturesque domed roofs of the bathhouses ensured that the steam ran down the walls rather than dripping onto the visitors. Nowadays bathers at the hammams can enjoy additional wellness services such as sauna, massages, or indoor swimming pools.

The Cultural Heritage

THE LEGACY OF THE SILK ROAD

The term "Silk Road" is not very old; the German geologist Ferdinand von Richthofen coined it in his scientific writings on the seven research trips he made through China between 1868 and 1872. No European since Marco Polo had travelled the country so thoroughly, and today the historic caravan route in general is known by this name. Not only goods for trading, but also ideas circulated along this route between Orient and Occident. Religions including Hinduism, Buddhism, Zoroastrianism, Christianity, and Islam were passed on. The Great Silk Road reached the zenith of its importance between the second century BC and the fifteenth century AD. From the mysterious Chinese Empire came silk and crops, paper, gunpowder, and porcelain; the West for its part could offer amber, coral, pewter, and glass.

The route was almost 12,800 kilometres in length and travelled from China and Japan through endless deserts and across almost impregnable mountain chains as far as southern and northern Europe. It consisted of a network of routes and subsidiary paths. Merchants and adventurers and soldiers of fortune would be on the road for up to eight years, unless they preferred to limit their travels to certain sections of the route. Vast profits beckoned, but the journey was a dangerous undertaking, so people travelled with escorts and in caravans with hundreds of horses and camels.

A side effect was the jobs this provided – for example, guards and camel drivers and money-changers were needed. Caravanserais – today often restored as accurately as possible and operated as historic hotels – served as lodgings and resting places for people and animals and also as storage places and shops. Settlements and bazaars grew into proper towns – or disappeared again when their rulers were usurped. Along the route, agricultural production sites and factories for ceramics, carpets, and silk weavers sprang up.

The Caucasus was part of the Great Silk Road and Azerbaijan was an important stopover with Baku, Basgal, Sheki, and Shamaki, among other locations. "Silk is produced in large quantities in Shamaki. Even the merchants from Genoa and Venice come here to purchase silk," confirmed the Castilian ambassador Ruiz Gonzales de Clavijo, and Ambrosio Contarini, a Venetian diplomat, praised the high quality of the silk produced in Shamaki during his visit there in the fifteenth century. Later it was not unusual to hear the names of towns like Sheki and Shamaki in Venetian coffeehouses,

and indeed Shamaki was one of the most important trading centres which exported large quantities of silk especially to Italy and France, as well as producing high-quality carpets. Metalworking, pottery, and weaving also played an important role. In the Middle Ages the little town of Basgal was much admired not only for its silk weaving, but also for its sewage system; every house was said to have its own bath.

The importance of the Great Silk Road declined after the discovery of the sea routes to India and America, but many of the well-preserved settlements are now integrated into the current tourist route along the historical Silk Road, and Azerbaijani craftsmen have taken up the tradition of their ancestors, so that silk and carpet weaving, metalworking, and pottery are enjoying a renaissance. Azerbaijan could play an important part once more as a part of the planned "New Great Silk Road" TRACECA, the Transport Corridor Europe – Caucasus – Asia.

THE NAGORNO-KARABAKH REGION

Nagorno-Karabakh is blessed with an ancient history and a valuable cultural heritage in literature, art, and music. Numerous examples of its folk art can be found in the world's most famous museums – in the Victoria and Albert Museum in London, the Louvre in Paris, the Metropolitan Museum of Art in New York, and many other museum collections in Vienna, Rome, Berlin, Istanbul, Teheran, and Cairo. The Karabakh region is also famous as a land of music; its centuries-old tradition has enriched the musical culture of Azerbaijan across the years. Precious carpets woven during various epochs in the Karabakh school of carpet weaving continue to fascinate people to this day with their beauty. The Heydar Aliyev Foundation provides energetic support for the maintenance of the spiritual and material heritage of Nagorno-Karabakh and aims to spread its fame throughout the world.

MUSIC

Mugham

Above all mugham, which is hundreds of years old, has always played an important role in the cultural tradition of Azerbaijan since earliest times. Its roots lie in Shirvan, Nakhichevan, Irevan, Tabriz, Ardabil, Hamadan, Mughan, and Karabakh – the cultural cradles of the former rural regions. Above all, Shusha, the capital of Nagorno-Karabakh, played a particularly important role in this context. It was here that mugham developed its present diversity from the second half of the eighteenth century onwards. Among the stars of the mugham school of Nagorno-Karabakh are the singer Jabbar Garyaghdioglu, the tar player Sadikchan, and the opera singer Bulbul. The philosophical and lyrical texts of mugham often stem from classical Azerbaijani poets such as Nizami or Fuzuli. Famous performers like Jabbar Karyaghdy, Sadigjan, and Bulbul are synonymous with this music. Traditionally the singer also determines the rhythm with the assistance of the frame drum, a sort of tambourine; he may also be accompanied by the tar (a long-necked lute) and the kamancheh (a bowed string instrument). Mughan has even made it as far as the stars! It travelled into space in 1977 on the golden disc on board the two Voyager probes as one of the examples of music on Earth. Since 2008 mugham has been on the UNESCO list of the oral and immaterial heritage of mankind. Mehriban Aliyeva, the First Lady of Azerbaijan and a UNESCO ambassador, opened an international mugham centre within the framework of the project "Eternal Mugham", which was started on the initiative of UNESCO and the Ministry for Culture and Tourism.

Jazz

In mugham the musicians improvise in turn on the theme provided according to strict rules. And so it is not surprising to find that it can be linked particularly well to jazz, which the state Estrade band made popular in Azerbaijan during the 1930s. The composer and pianist Vagif Mustafazadeh, who died at an early age, became a supreme master in the symbiosis of jazz and mugham, thereby creating a new musical genre. The jazz trumpeter Dizzie Gillespie described him as a great genius but said that he was born too soon for his futuristic music.

Aziza Vagif Mustafazadeh, Vagif's daughter, who lives mostly in Germany, won the Thelonious Monk Piano Competition at the age of only 17 in Washington and is world famous as a jazz musician. Ultimately, she is continuing the tradition of Azerbaijan, where there have been female composers, musicians, and singers since the Middle Ages.

The Classical Tradition

First recordings of Azerbaijani music could be found in Germany as early as the end of the nineteenth century. It quickly gained an international profile after it became possible to create a form of notation for the music at the beginning of the twentieth century. Azerbaijani, Oriental and Western musical elements are frequently combined. The first Muslim opera, *Layla and Majnum*, also originated in Azerbaijan and had its première in Baku in 1908. It is based on the work *Layla and Majnum*, composed in 1907 by Uzeyir Hajibeyov, by Nizami, the national poet, which was written between 1180 and 1188, a subject which in his turn Fuzuli, the great Azerbaijani poet of the sixteenth century, also took up. His masterpiece *Layla and Majnum* provided the basis for the libretto of the opera. Its composer, Uzeyir bey Abdul Huseyn Hajibeyli (1885–1948), was the founder of the national composition school and the state conservatory, and he was the first composer to create genres like opera, operetta, chamber music, piano compositions, cantatas, and songs in the Muslim world of the Orient. His operetta *Arshin Mal Alan* was translated into more than 60 languages and has been very successfully presented internationally, including in 2006 at the Kammeroper in Vienna under the title *The Cloth Peddler*.

A student of Uzeyir Hajibeyli, Gara Garayev, was influenced by the Second Viennese School around Arnold Schönberg and continued the tradition of composers like Dmitri Shostakovich and Sergei Prokofiev. Frangiz Ali-Zadeh has been very successful. Born in Baku in 1947, following her studies at the conservatory in the early 1970s, the female composer and pianist initially worked in her home town and later in Turkey. She moved to Berlin in 1999 with a DAAD scholarship. She has taken part amongst other things within the framework of the Silk Road Project and has performed in Carnegie Hall. Today she lives in Azerbaijan and is the chairperson on the Association of Composers of the Republic of Azerbaijan.

Each year the international Mstislav Rostropovich Festival is held in Baku, the home town of the world-famous cellist. The artistic director is the cellist's daughter Olga Rostropovich. Here not only famous orchestras, ensembles, and soloists from all over the world come together; young artists also have the opportunity to present their virtuosity or to perform the première of their works.

Pop and Popular Music

In 2011 the Azerbaijani duo Ell & Nikki won the Eurovision Song Contest in Düsseldorf with their contribution "Running Scared". The contest was therefore held in Baku in 2012; to stage it, the spectacular Crystal Palace was specially built on a spit of land.

LITERATURE

The high esteem in which Azerbaijan holds its poets is unmistakable. They greet visitors as larger-than-life-sized statues in Baku at the National Library and the Palace of Literature, which was built in 1860 and used from 1914/15 as the Hotel Metropol before being rebuilt to mark the Nizami Year 1940/41. They are also honoured in many other towns with monuments or street names.

Nizami Ganjavi (ca. 1141–1209), whom Goethe had called the "teacher of all poets", wrote the *Chamsa*, five epic poems whose "delicate, highly skilled spirit…, which chooses the most attractive interdependencies of most sincere love as the subject of his poems, …" deeply impressed Goethe. The poetry of the poet and philosopher Nasimi (1369–1417) was rooted in the social, political, and cultural tradition of the countries of the Near and Middle East. Nasimi wrote in Azerbaijani-Turkish (Old Anatolian), Persian, and Arabic. His poems were also translated into German; in 2012 the Heydar Aliyev Foundation published a book about Nasimi's poetry in French. As a supporter of Hurufism, a sect given to mystical speculations, he was flayed alive as a heretic. With the participation of UNESCO Nasimi's 600th anniversary was celebrated in several cities throughout the world.

The English Orientalist Elias John Wilkinson Gibb referred to another outstanding representative of Azerbaijani literature, Muhammad Fuzuli (1494–1556), a "poet of the soul". He achieved fame above all with his love story *Layla and Majnum*, an oriental version of *Romeo and Juliet*.

Women writers can look back on a rich tradition in the literature of Azerbaijan. As early as the twelfth century, Mehseti Genjevi (1089–1159) achieved fame as a musician and was the first woman to play chess. Above all, however, she was one of the country's greatest women poets. Khurshidbanu Natavan (1832–97), the daughter of the last Chan of Karabakh, was not only a highly esteemed lyric poet during the nineteenth century; she also produced the finest embroidery, and decorated a tobacco pouch, amongst other items. When Alexandre Dumas visited the Caucasus, he was delighted to receive it as a gift.

In his home town of Peine, Friedrich von Bodenstedt can be seen sitting on a bench – as a bronze sculpture. Bodenstedt had originally published his translation of the *Songs of Mirza Shafi* (1794–1852), one of the most widely purchased books during the nineteenth century, as a collection of oriental poems by his language teacher Mirza Shafi from Tiflis, in whose house he had sojourned for a long time. Some 25 years after they were first published, von Bodenstedt announced that he was the author, a fact which was doubted by many at the time.

Azerbaijan was one of the first Muslim countries to integrate Western literary forms. At the beginning of the twentieth century, authors like Jalil Mammadguluzadeh (1862–1911) provided new impetus. He was the publisher of the magazine *Molla Nasraddin*, in which he published satires against feudal backwardness. His colleagues included Mirza Alakbar Sabir (1862–1911), who amongst other things satirised the rapid acquisition of wealth through petroleum; Huseyn Javid (1882–1941), a humanist philosopher and Romantic who became a victim of Stalinist repression; and also Jafar Jabbarly (1899–1934), whose works frequently took as their subject the emancipation of women.

A modern classic and bestseller is *Ali and Nino*, a love story between an Azerbaijani and a woman from Georgia shortly before the First World War. The author was Leo Nussimbaum, born in Baku and resident in Germany – a colourful character whose books about the Orient, written during the 1920s and 1930s under the pseudonyms Kurban Said and Essad Bey, achieved unprecedented sales success.

Apart from new translations of classics like the works of Nizamim, contemporary authors are also very popular. They include Bakhtiyar Vahabzadeh (1925–2009), who in particular championed literature in Turkish, and Mir Jalal Pashayev (1908–1978), whose acute powers of observation enabled him to portray the characters of people and the society in which they lived.

Anar Rzayev is also very popular. In his novel *The Sixth Floor of the Five-Story Building* he describes a love affair which is doomed because of the traditions of society. His books were translated into several European languages as well as into Arabic and the languages of the former Soviet Union and were published in many countries. The problems of relationships amongst people of different religions and nationalities were also examined by Elchin Afandiyev in his novel *Mahmud and Marjam*; his works also include *White Camel*, which achieved fame as a film adaptation.

THE TEMPLE OF FIRE

Since earliest times, people have been fascinated by Azerbaijan's fire, which flares up directly out of the ground. Across the centuries it attracted hermits and pilgrims, who ascribed a cultic importance to the flames and built temples. It seems likely that the Zoroastrians also used the Temple of Fire at Ateshgah, which was dedicated to Jvala Ji, the Hindu goddess of fire. Indians living in Baku had built it in several stages between the seventeenth and early nineteenth centuries. Its purpose was to serve the religious needs of the Indian merchants who travelled around in this region and who were both Hindus and Sikhs.

Inscriptions have been found on numerous walls and gates; most are in Devanagari alphabet, while two are in Gurmukhī alphabet and one in Persian-Arabic. The complex is surrounded by a defiant pentagonal wall in which the priests' cells and lodgings for pilgrims were located. In the middle of the courtyard stands the temple, which is open on all sides. Its eternal flames are fed by natural gas, which, however, flows through pipes nowadays. The site was abandoned at the end of the nineteenth century, when oil production began nearby; in 1975 it was turned into a museum.

YEDDI GUNBAZ

Mausoleum of the Seven Domes in Shamakhi

You never know whether the city will still be standing tomorrow, wrote Alexandre Dumas. Indeed, attacks and devastating earthquakes destroyed Shamakhi, which was mentioned by Claudius Ptolemy as early as the second century, on several occasions. They even led to the capital of the former Kingdom of Shirvan-shah being moved to Baku after yet another disastrous quake during the twelfth century. The mausoleums of Yeddi Gunbaz – Seven Domes – serve several dynasties as burial place. Begun in the eighteenth century and later extended, they continue to bear traces of the damage: the gravestones, some of which have been overturned, rise out of the ground at bizarre angles, and not all seven domes have survived. The town lies 135 kilometres northwest of Baku amongst idyllic hills on which wine is traditionally grown.

THE TOWN OF SHEKI

Sheki, one of the most attractive and oldest small towns in rural Azerbaijan, lies in the mountainous North. Its inhabitants are open-minded and friendly. The Summer Palace of Khans, built during the second half of the eighteenth century, is one of the most important sights in the country. The outer walls of the two-storey residence, which lies in an idyllic park, are decorated with elaborate tiled ornamentation and artistic windows of stained glass. To create these, countless panes of coloured glass were mounted accurately to the last millimetre into a fine framework of battens without the use of nails or glue. This unique craft is known as "shebeke" (from the Arabic word meaning "net"). The walls inside are decorated almost completely with coloured paintings of hunting and war scenes as well as flowers and especially birds. The ornamentation of the palace has been used as decoration on some of the pages of this book.

Caravanserais in Sheki

A visit to the upper and lower caravanserais of Sheki is like a journey back into olden times. In the two-storey arcaded building dating from the eighteenth century and in the rooms which lie behind and the magnificent inner courtyard, travellers along the Silk Road used to find comfortable lodgings in which to rest. Today the upper caravanserai is a modern but romantic hotel with an attached restaurant and banqueting hall.

THE CHURCH OF KISH

The land that extends from the Greater Caucasus as far as the Kura and Aras rivers and which roughly corresponds to what today is the Republic of Azerbaijan was mentioned for the first time in Greek sources in the fourth century BC. In those days it was called Albania (not to be confused with Albania in the Balkans). In the Hellenic Period, roughly towards the end of the second century BC, it seems that a number of tribes joined together under a single leader. They fought against Alexander the Great and were defeated in 65 BC by Gnaeus Pompeius (Pompey). In the third century AD they took part in the war against the Persians as vassals of Rome, and so were exposed to influences from Persian, Hellenist, and Roman culture. The Albanian ruler Urnayr (313–371) declared Christianity to be the state religion after he was said to have been baptised by St Gregory. Arabs arrived in the region during the seventh century. The region of Azerbaijani Albania was not completely Islamised at this stage, however. Instead, Christians probably remained in the towns until well into the tenth century.

In Kish, a few kilometres north of Sheki, stands a simple little church. When it was being restored within the framework of an Azerbaijani-Norwegian joint project in which Thor Heyerdahl was involved, ceramics from the Kura-Araxes Culture were found here. These indicate that a cult site was located here as early as about 3,000 BC. Among the finds from the Christian Era were a little mother-of-pearl cross, gold threads, and a buckle of embossed gold, probably from the garments of priests and dating from the fourteenth century. Radiocarbon analyses indicate that the church was built between 990 and 1160 AD. Today it is a museum.

LAHIJ

A Village in Ismailli

The village of Lahij, which is protected as a cultural monument, lies tucked away in the Caucasus Mountains at a height of 1375 metres. The hazardous gravelled road which leads there is due to be modernised, but many tourists already visit the town, because of its original flair. On the car park outside the town children and young people offer items for sale, and saddled horses invite visitors to a leisurely tour of the town on horseback. In alleys paved with rough cobblestones, dimly lit shops offer carpets and authentic handicrafts for sale. You can browse through the coppersmiths' stores for which Lahij is especially famous and purchase dishes, samovars, and items with metal ornamentation after watching the coppersmith at work. The women meet at the water hole, chatting and washing the laundry as they do so. An intensive mixture of oriental aromas will guide you towards the stores of the spice merchants with their brightly coloured delicacies, dried flowers and herbs. Time seems to have stood still in Lahij.

KHINALIG

A Village in Guba

As a result of its earlier remoteness and with a history reaching back over 5,000 years, Khinalig is considered one of the oldest inhabited settlements in the world. The houses are built of dark grey stone and clay, against which window frames, doors and the gutters gleam sky blue and snow white.

In one of her watercolours, the Azerbaijani painter Maral Rahmanzadeh (1916–2008) reduced the spectacular highest village in the country (at an altitude of 2,350 metres) to its rough charm: houses crowd in on each other on a lofty mountain, perched against the backdrop of even taller, more majestic mountains. Nowadays they lure increasing numbers of mountaineers, thereby enabling the young locals to earn their living as guides. Only a few years ago, Khinalig was only accessible for three months a year. With the construction of a better road this has changed; electricity has also arrived on the scene in Khinalig, while satellite television is further contributing towards linking the town with the rest of the world. However, this also means that its unique language, Ketsh, which has been handed down orally through the generations, is endangered. In 1895 Roderich von Erckert, a German Lieutenant General, was the first to study the idiom, which belongs to the Northeastern Caucasian group of languages in greater detail; the German philologist and ethnologist Adolf Dirr drew up the first accounts of its structure. The written language was determined in the 1960s by a team of Russian philologists; Ketsh is now being researched further by Tamrika Khvtisiashvili, supported, amongst other sponsors, by the DoBes Volkswagen Foundation and the government of Azerbaijan. By means of targeted teaching it should prove possible to prevent the complete loss of the language, which would otherwise occur within just two generations.

The Markets

ORIENTAL AND COLOURFUL

Plump fresh fruits and wrinkled dried fruits; appetising piles of crisp vegetables; delicate flower petals, syrups, and sauces; the assorted aromas of colourful spices and herbs; and crowds of people pushing and shoving – there can be no doubt that Azerbaijan is one of the most fertile countries on Earth and that here you are in an oriental market. Live chickens, their legs tied together, crouch in a chest beside the fresh-meat stall, and the merchants and customers, a noticeable number of whom are men, talk knowledgeably at the cheese stand with its variety of home-made cheeses and over the smoked fish of all sizes.

The merchants are mostly also the producers and present their seasonal fruit and vegetables with great pride. Of course nothing is wasted of the ample harvest, and so preserves are also offered all the year round. Cornelian cherries, for example, which are rarely planted and harvested in Germany, are very popular in Azerbaijan. They are used to produce fruit schnapps, and with the addition of large amounts of sugar are also made into jam.

Every town and village has its own market; many of them are roofed over. In one of the halls, household goods are offered for sale, from besoms to bright pink buckets, not to mention tools, nails, screws, and light bulbs, while in the next you will find flowers and plants; and in the one after that, songbirds, cats, dogs, donkeys, and sheep wait for new owners. The "antique" shops in remote corners are real treasure troves where you can barter for ceramic dishes, oil lamps, and caskets.

There are several markets in Baku. The "Teze Bazaar" is one of the markets in the centre. The name means "New Bazaar", although it has long been one of the "old" ones. Here you will even find delicacies like sturgeon and caviar, which are otherwise only found in very exclusive food shops. The "Oriental Bazaar", a short distance outside the town, is a paradise for fruit and vegetables.

CAVIAR

At the beginning of the twentieth century, France's famous chef Auguste Escoffier described caviar as "without doubt the most exclusive and subtle of all hors d'oeuvres." Five hundred years previously, his compatriot Bertrandon de la Broquière voiced a very different opinion during his journey through Asia Minor; in 1431 he wrote that unless one had nothing else to eat, "cavyaire" was at best fit only for the Greeks. Cervantes, on the other hand, added a "black delicacy called cavial" to an alfresco meal in his novel Don Quijote; and in 1797 Friedrich Gottlob Leonhardi described in his *Erdbeschreibung der Preußischen Monarchie* the sturgeon shack in Alt Pillau, where "sturgeon that had been caught ... and caviar ... were prepared and packed ...". He commented that a large sturgeon "gives up to... 12 pots of caviar, which is as good as the Russian variety." In the "Instructions for the preparation of caviar from a letter by the medicinal assessor and pharmacist Michaelis zu Magdeburg", the author emphasises that the popular cold dish was only prepared in a few places, namely Pillau, Magdeburg, and Cologne, although a "well-run factory could become a profitable businesss for several regions within the fatherland."

The "profitable" business with the "black gold of the tsars" – 50 fishermen were employed to provide Peter the Great with fresh caviar at all times – has long since declined dramatically as a result of overfishing and environmental pollution. The coastal states bordering the Caspian Sea, where the four species of sturgeon that are most important for the caviar trade live, have reached an agreement that from 2014 they will not be allowed to catch sturgeon for a period of five years.

As a result, the farming of sturgeon and the production of caviar in aquaculture is becoming progressively more interesting for Azerbaijan. Throughout the country there are a number of operations in which sturgeon is cultured: in the facility in Khilly alone, there are some 15 million young sturgeon. The modern equipment there also permits the roe to be removed from the live fish, so that they can be used several times for the removal of roe. Spawners of various species of sturgeon are taken to their breeding grounds and the young fish that hatch there are later released in the estuaries of the Caspian Sea.

The "milking" of caviar from live sturgeon using a specially developed procedure has been patented worldwide by the Alfred Wegener Institute for Polar and Marine Research in Bremerhaven.

They are in any case getting very close to their ideal. Farmed caviar should taste as far as possible like top-quality wild caviar – creamy, buttery, and nutty – and the grains should glow amber coloured, gold-brown, or mid- to steel grey.

Of course this delicacy, served for preference on fine crystal and tasted with a spoon of mother-of-pearl or horn, should only be served with ice-cold vodka or Champagne.

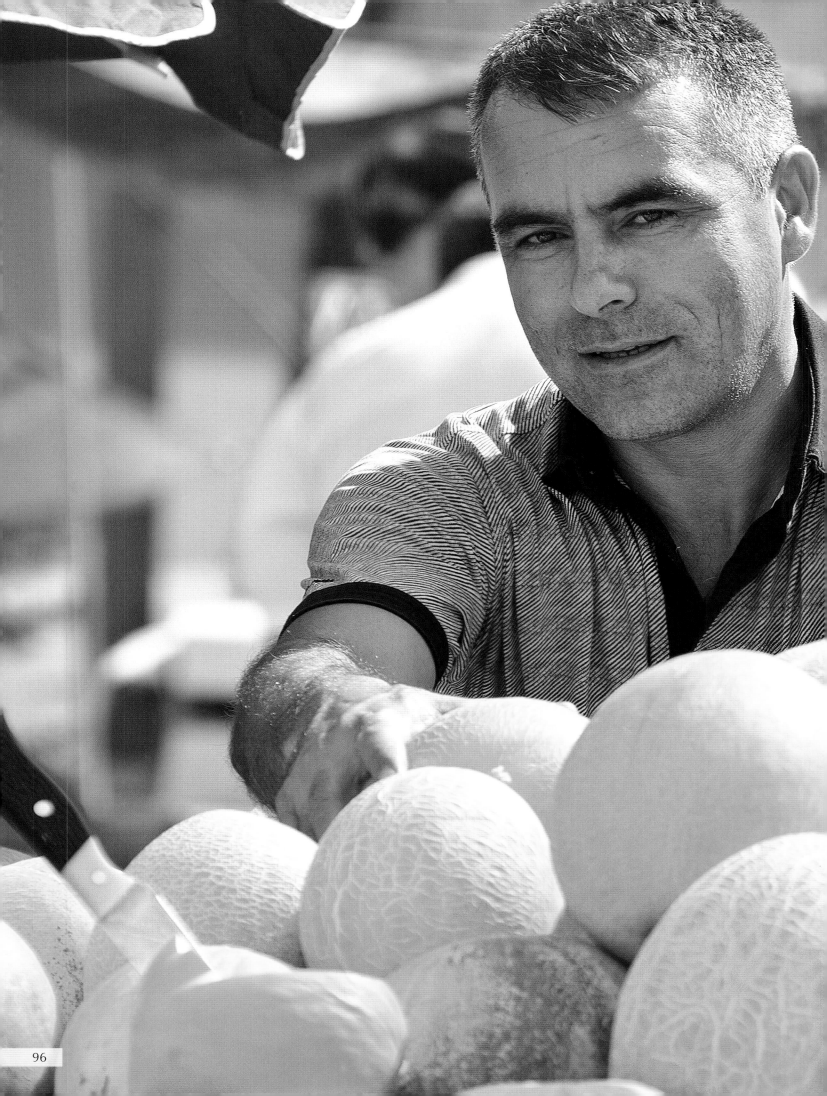

CHEESE

The basis for qatiq (yoghurt) and kesmik (curd cheese) is cow's, sheep's and goat's milk as well as buffalo's milk, which is especially prized. Soured milk and a pendir, which is reminiscent of feta, is also popular. Qurut has a particularly intense flavour; it consists of balls of kesmik which are rolled in salt whilst still damp to prevent mould; thereafter they can be kept for several months. Another aromatic cheese is shor, a granular cheese. It is produced by bringing milk to the boil and then adding a small quantity of qatik to make it curdle; the curdled milk is then passed through a cheesecloth. Like motal pendiri it acquires a special flavour because it is allowed to mature in a wineskin made of sheep's leather. Rennet cheese is made of sheep's milk, sometimes mixed with goat's milk; it is produced by the addition of rennet from newborn lambs, or of lady's bedstraw. Sachaq pendir, a smoked cheese often presented in the form of a plait, tastes particularly good with beer.

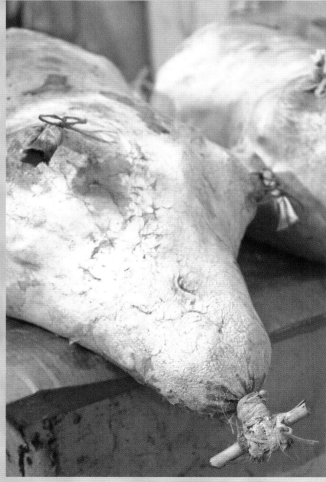

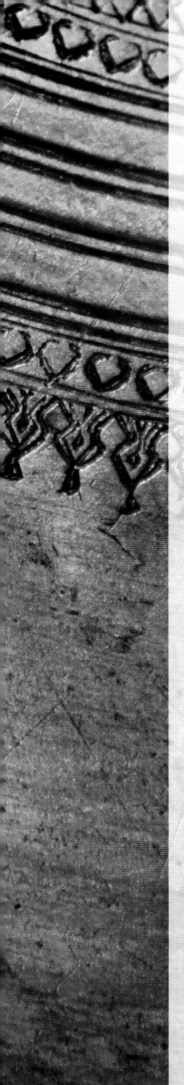

The Cuisine of Azerbaijan

The warm climate and fertile soil permit fruit and vegetables to thrive in abundance throughout the country. Cattle and sheep can move freely on the vast open spaces, thereby creating ideal conditions for excellent food products.

The meal begins with a wide range of small hors d'oeuvres; fresh herbs and dovga, a yoghurt soup, are essential components. A favourite of Azerbaijani national cuisine is known as plov, a rice dish which can be prepared in a variety of ways. Shah Plov is a festive dish for which rice flavoured with saffron, lamb, dates, and chestnuts is baked in pastry and served with a crisp crust. Meat and vegetables are often served with yoghurt, which lends the dish a fresh flavour and which is particularly welcome on hot days. Kebabs, the familiar form of grilled meat, are very popular and are served with delicious side dishes including fresh vegetables and savoury sauces, often flavoured with pomegranates or plums, which lend them an aromatic sweet-and-sour note. An essential feature of the selection of hors d'oeuvres are dolmas, for which a seasoned stuffing of minced lamb is wrapped in pistachio or vine leaves or cabbage. Dolmas are also frequently served in a pastry case or arranged on pieces of pasta dough and seasoned with a fruit sauce.

Thanks to the abundance of fish stocks in the Caspian Sea, of course fish dishes play an important role. Balik, grilled sturgeon served on a skewer, is a speciality served with a fruit sauce. In Azerbaijan, bughlama refers to the method of preparation: it is a dish prepared with only a small amount of liquid and is served with a side dish of vegetables and herbs. Caspian kutum or carp are filled with walnuts, onions, and spices and are then baked in the oven.

In addition to locally produced wines, Azerbaijanis enjoy drinking sherbet, a sweet, cold fruit juice often laced with mint. There are many different varieties of sherbet. The most popular include those made with lemon, pomegranate, strawberry, cherry, and apricot. The variety of types of fruit is striking: strawberries, blackberries, figs, watermelon, apricots, cherries, plums, walnuts, and even fragrant rose petals.

Sweet dishes are particularly popular in this Oriental cuisine. Tea from the samovar appears on the table at every opportunity, together with different kinds of jam, which is eaten straight from the spoon, without bread. A table prepared for such a meal is not only a culinary delight for the guest; it is also an attractive sight. Shekerburas are a typical baked dish: they are small decorated croissant-shaped baked goods filled with a mixture of sugar and nuts and are traditionally served at the annual Nowruz festival. In addition to an endless variety of other sweet delicacies, a type of baklava and so-called ordubad rolls, sweet rolls of pastry that have been cut open, occupy a firm place in the cuisine of Azerbaijan.

Mutton fat is traditionally added to most Azerbaijani dishes. Clarified butter is a good substitute and is used in the recipes described in this book. A modern, contemporary cuisine aims, however, to make less use of animal fats and so vegetable oil can be used in all recipes instead of clarified butter.

Baked Walnuts with Eggs

Kuku

Serves 6 / 30 minutes

200–300 g walnuts
2 large onions
5–6 eggs
1 tbsp flour
Salt
Freshly ground black pepper
2 tbsp clarified butter or vegetable oil

And also:
2 tbsp Sumach
Freshly chopped flat-leaf parsley or coriander according to taste

Coarsely chop 100 g walnuts and finely grind the rest. Peel and chop the onions very finely, either with a food chopper or a knife. Place the chopped onions on a clean tea towel or muslin cloth and press to remove the juice. Put the walnuts, onions, eggs, and flour in a bowl, mix well and season with salt and pepper.

Heat 1 tbsp clarified butter or oil in a frying pan. Add the egg and walnut mixture, cover and allow to set over a low heat. When the surface of the mass is also cooked, tip the Kuku onto a flat plate. Heat another 1 tbsp clarified butter or oil in a frying pan and briefly fry the Kuku from the other side.

Line a large plate with baking paper and turn out the cooked Kuku. Sprinkle with chopped herbs and serve with Sumach to season according to taste. Kuku can also be eaten cold.

Tip

You can also bake Kuku in the oven in a suitable baking dish.

Filled Vine Leaves

Yarpaq dolması

Serves 4 / 40 minutes

2 large onions
1 sprig each of flat-leaf parsley, dill,
mint, and coriander
100 g round-grain rice
500 g minced lamb (alternatively:
minced beef or veal)
Salt
Freshly ground black pepper
250–300 g vine leaves (fresh or marinated)

And also:
250 g plain yoghurt
2 large cloves garlic

Peel the onions and chop finely in the chopper or with a sharp knife. Wash the herbs, shake them dry, and chop finely. Wash the rice. Mix the onions, herbs, and rice with the minced lamb, season with salt and pepper and mix thoroughly.

Remove the stalks of the vine leaves. Bring some water to the boil in a saucepan and blanch the vine leaves briefly. Lay the blanched leaves on a shallow plate or spread out in a pile on a teatowel.

Place 1 heaped tbsp of the minced meat in the centre of each leaf, roll up like a beef olive or fold together firmly to create a square package. Pack the dolmas tightly into a pan and weight down with a flat plate (smaller than the pan) so that they do not come apart whilst cooking. Half-fill the pan with cold water and cook the dolmas over a low heat for up to 1 hour. If the water evaporates too fast, add a little more hot water and continue to simmer. Remove the plate carefully.

Press the garlic through the garlic press and mix with the yoghurt.

Serve the dolmas in a deep dish, adding a little of the cooking liquid. Serve with the garlic-yoghurt sauce and fresh bread.

Colourful stands crop up frequently along the country roads, between the trees. They offer for sale whatever the local farmers can produce – fresh fruit and vegetables, flowers, juices, schnapps, syrup, jam, nuts, and dried fruits. The Azerbaijanis are experts when it comes to preserving the produce from their bounteous harvests. Preserved sour fruits or vegetables are particularly decorative. They are mostly filled into the large preserving jars which are stacked up almost wall-high, creating a tantalising artwork and a feast for the senses.

Sour Preserved Fruit and Vegetables

Turshu

For preserved fruit:
e.g. mirabelles, cherries, crab apples, cornel cherries

For preserved vegetables:
e.g. ridge cucumbers, cherry tomatoes, pumpkin, carrots, cauliflower

And also:
Salt
250 ml white wine vinegar per litre of water
1 bay leaf per jar
½ tbsp peppercorns per jar
½ tbsp coriander seeds per jar
Fresh flat-leaf parsley and dill
Fresh vine leaves
Preserving jars

Wash the fruit and drain but do not remove the stones. Pack the fruit into the clean preserving jars according to size. Add the bay leaf, peppercorns, and coriander seeds.

Put the water, salt, and white wine vinegar in a pan and bring to the boil, then allow to cool down to room temperature. Fill the jars with the pickling liquid and cover with the lid, but do not seal yet.

Half-fill a wide, deep pan with water and bring it to the boil (or use preserving apparatus). Place the jars in the pan and sterilise for 20-30 minutes. The jars should be two-thirds immersed in water. Immediately seal the jars, turn them upside down, and leave until they have cooled down completely.

Wash and trim the vegetables. Cut away the stalk and core of the pumpkin, carrots, and cauliflower and cut into pieces. Fill the jars either with single varieties or with a mixture of vegetables and then proceed as for the preserved fruit. In addition, in the case of the vegetables you can also add parsley, dill, and fresh vine leaves according to taste.

Grilled Minced Meat

Lyula-Kebab

Serves 4 / 40 minutes

2 medium-sized onions
500 g minced meat – not too lean (minced lamb, beef, or veal)
Salt
Freshly ground black pepper
4 tomatoes
1 onion
1 bouquet coriander (alternatively: dill)
1 tbsp sumach
Fresh flatbread

And also:
Wooden skewers

For the meat, peel the onions and chop very finely in the food chopper or with a knife. Add the meat and mix everything well using the chopper or your hands. Season with salt and pepper. Form the meat mixture into balls, cover and chill for approx. 30 minutes in the fridge.

Pre-heat the oven on the grill setting to maximum heat or prepare the charcoal grill. Moisten your hands with water, form the meat mixture into sausages, and place on skewers. Grill the kebabs on all sides for 10–15 minutes on the charcoal grill or in the oven.

Wash the tomatoes; depending on size, cut into quarters or eighths and put them on 4 skewers, too. Peel the onions and cut into fine rings. Wash the coriander, shake dry and pluck coarsely.

Lay the flatbread on a place, arrange the kebabs on top and garnish with onion rings, tomato pieces, and coriander. Finally sprinkle the sumach over the dish before serving.

Filled Pancakes

Gutab

Serves 4 / 50 minutes

For the meat filling:
1 large onion
300 g minced meat (minced lamb, beef, or veal)
Salt
Freshly ground black pepper

For the pumpkin filling:
½ Hokkaido squash
1 medium-sized onion
30 g clarified butter
Cinnamon

For the herb filling:
2–3 sprigs each dill, chives, coriander, spinach, parsley

For the pancakes:
500 g flour
1 egg
Salt

And also:
Flour for rolling out
Butter for spreading
Sumach
Yoghurt
1–2 sprigs dill or other herbs

To make the meat filling, peel the onion, chop very finely and mix thoroughly with the minced meat. Season with salt and pepper.

For the pumpkin filling, wash the pumpkin, remove the stalk, and cut into small pieces. Put in a saucepan with a little water and cook until tender. Peel and chop the onion. Heat the clarified butter in a frying pan and fry the onions until golden brown. Mix the cooked pumpkin with the fried onions, season with salt and cinnamon, and mash with a fork.

For the herb filling, wash the herbs and shake dry, then chop on a chopping board. Season the chopped herbs with salt and pepper to taste.

Mix the flour, egg, salt, and water to make a firm dough, divide into 12 pieces and form each into a ball. Using a rolling pin, roll out the balls of dough to form a circle. The dough should be as thin as possible (approx. 2 mm).

Put the prepared fillings on one half of each circle of dough, fold over the other half and press the edges firmly together. Fry the pancakes on both sides in a pre-heated frying pan.

Spread butter on the gutab whilst they are still hot; sprinkle them with sumach.

Serve the gutab with herb filling with yoghurt. Serve the other gutab with additional sumach.

Tip:

In order to speed up the frying process, you can put a little oil in the frying pan. You can also sprinkle pomegranate seeds on the meat and pumpkin fillings.

Soup with Filled Pasta

Dushbara

Serves 4 / 60 minutes

For the soup:
500 g boiling meat with bones (e.g. lamb or beef)
1 medium-sized onion
2 tbsp clarified butter
Salt
Freshly ground black pepper
1 tbsp dried mint

For the filling:
200 g minced meat (minced lamb, beef, or veal)
1 medium-sized onion
1 tbsp fresh dill

For the pasta:
150 g flour
1 egg

And also:
Flour for the work surface
1–2 cloves garlic per person
White wine vinegar

For the soup, put the meat in a saucepan with 1 ½ l water (the meat should be just covered) and simmer gently over a low heat for approx. 60 minutes. Skim off any scum that rises to the top using a ladle. Pour off the stock. Peel the onion and chop very finely. Heat the clarified butter in a large pan and gently fry the onions until they are transparent. Pour on the stock, season with salt and pepper, and put to the side.

In the meantime, chop the onion for the filling very finely, using a chopper or a sharp knife. Mix with the minced meat and the herbs and season with salt and pepper.

To make the pasta dough, knead together the flour, egg, a little salt, and lukewarm water. The dough should be smooth and firm. On a floured work surface, roll out the dough thinly (approx.1 mm) and cut into small squares approx. 2 x 2 cm. Place ½ tsp minced meat on each of the squares and fold them in half diagonally to make a triangle, pressing the edges together to seal and form small pockets.

Bring the soup back to the boil, reduce the heat and allow the little pasta triangles to simmer in the broth. The *dushbara* are cooked as soon as they rise to the surface. Adjust the seasoning with salt and pepper if required and sprinkle over the dried mint.

This dish is served as a soup together with the other hors d'oeuvres. At wish, the soup can be seasoned additionally at the table with crushed garlic and white wine vinegar.

Tip:

You can also use a pasta machine to roll out the dough.

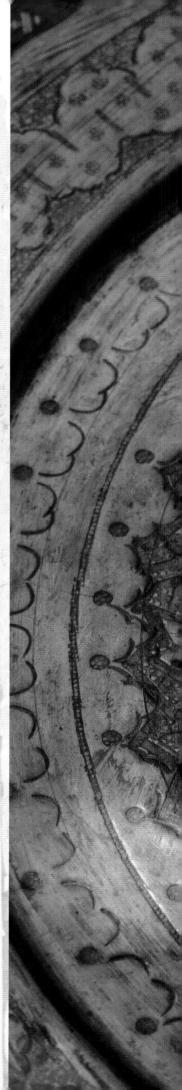

Green Beans with Eggs

Chighirtma Lobya

Serves 4 / 30 minutes

1 kg green runner beans
2 onions
2 large tomatoes
Salt
Freshly ground black pepper
½ tsp ground cumin
Freshly chopped herbs
(mint, parsley, dill, coriander, basil)
4–5 eggs
150 g clarified butter or vegetable oil

Trim and wash the beans and cut into pieces approx. 2–2.5 cm in length. Bring a large pan of salted water to the boil and cook the beans al dente for approx. 2–3 minutes. Drain. Make a crosswise slit in the tomatoes with a sharp knife, scald them with boiling water, remove the skins and cut the flesh into small pieces. Peel and finely chop the onions.

Heat the oil or clarified butter in a large, deep frying pan. Gently fry the onions over a medium heat until they are golden, then add the beans and tomatoes, and simmer until the liquid has evaporated. Stir from time to time and finally add the chopped herbs. Season with salt and pepper.

Beat the eggs in a bowl, season lightly with salt and pepper, and whisk again. Pour evenly over the vegetables, cover with a lid and leave for a few minutes until the eggs have set.

Break up the egg and bean mixture with a fork and serve straight from the pan with crusty white bread.

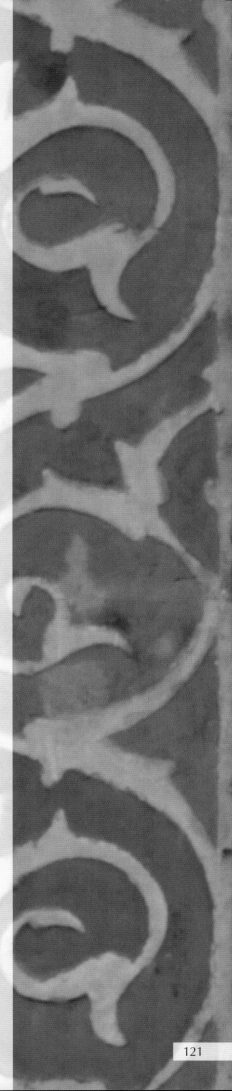

Stuffed Aubergines, Tomatoes, and Peppers

Dolma

Serves 4 / 40 minutes

4 long, slender aubergines
4 large beef tomatoes
4 medium-sized green bell peppers
3 medium-sized onions
Vegetable oil
500 g minced meat (minced lamb, beef, or veal)
Salt
Freshly ground black pepper
A bouquet each of fresh red basil, parsley, mint, dill, and coriander
250 g plain yoghurt
2–3 cloves garlic

Bring a pan of salted water to the boil. Remove the stalks of the aubergines and slit open each aubergine lengthways. Put the aubergines in the boiling water and simmer for 2–3 minutes, remove from the water and leave to cool. If the aubergines have a lot of seeds, rinse them out under running water.

Cut a lid from the top of the tomatoes and scoop out the flesh. Save the lid and the flesh. Do the same with the peppers, removing the seeds and the core.

Peel and finely chop the onions. Chop the flesh from the tomatoes. Heat some vegetable oil in a pan and lightly fry together with the minced meat, stirring continuously. The meat should not be fully cooked but should remain moist. Remove from the stove and season with salt and pepper. Wash the herbs and shake dry, chop and add to the meat. Mix everything thoroughly.

Season the inside of the vegetables with salt and pepper, fill with the meat and lay side by side in a wide pan. Place the lids on the tomatoes and peppers. Add ½ cup water, cover and braise over a medium heat until the liquid has evaporated and the vegetables are tender.

Press the cloves of garlic through the garlic press and stir into the yoghurt.

For each person, arrange an aubergine, a pepper, and a tomato on a plate and serve with fresh flatbread and the garlic-flavoured yoghurt.

Tip:

The meat can also be flavoured with cinnamon and the yoghurt mixed with cinnamon instead of garlic.

Filled Aubergine

Levengi

Serves 4 / 40 minutes

For the rolls:
2 large aubergines
Salt
3 tbsp vegetable oil
Freshly ground black pepper

For the filling:
1 medium-sized onion
2–3 tbsp clarified butter
200 g finely chopped walnuts
5–6 tbsp pomegranate syrup

And also:
Dried cornel cherries
Mayonnaise

Wash the aubergines and cut off the stalks. Slice thinly using a sharp knife or a slicing machine. Heat the vegetable oil in a frying pan and fry the aubergines until golden on both sides. Pat dry with kitchen paper and season again with salt and pepper.

For the filling, peel the onion and chop very finely. Heat the clarified butter in a deep frying pan and gently fry the onions over a medium heat until golden yellow. Add the chopped nuts. Continue to fry for about 5 more minutes, stirring continuously. Add the pomegranate syrup and mix well. Season with salt and pepper.

Spread 1 tbsp filling on each aubergine slice and roll up to make a roll.

Arrange the aubergine rolls on a plate – e.g. on a bed of dried cornel cherries, add some mayonnaise at wish, and serve as a cold hors d'oeuvre.

Tip:

You can vary the filling by mixing the nuts with a crushed clove of garlic and 3–4 tbsp mayonnaise before spreading it on the aubergine slices. In this case the filling does not need to be fried. After rolling them up, arrange the rolls on a plate and decorate with mayonnaise and chopped nuts.

Aubergine Puree

Badimjan ezmesi

Serves 4 / 50 minutes

3–4 large aubergines
3–4 red peppers
3–4 medium-sized tomatoes
2–3 sprigs each of basil, flat-leaf parsley, mint,
coriander, and dill
1 medium-sized onion
2 spring onions
Juice of ½ lemon
Salt
Freshly ground black pepper

Preheat the oven to 180° C / 350° F (upper and lower heat). Wash the vegetables and pat them dry. Wash the herbs and shake them dry. Pierce the skins of the aubergines and peppers a few times with a fork. Then place them with the tomatoes on a baking tray and cook in the oven until tender. Remove from the oven, and whilst the vegetables are still hot, remove the skin of the aubergines, skin the peppers and remove the core and seeds; skin the tomatoes. Leave to cool.

While the vegetables are in the oven, peel and finely dice the onion. Finely chop the herbs and the spring onions. Reserve 1 tbsp to garnish and put the rest with the chopped onions in a bowl.

Then coarsely chop the vegetables or mash them with a fork; mix with the other ingredients and season with lemon juice, salt, and pepper.

Aubergine puree is a popular hors d'oeuvre or side dish. It is served cold with bread as an accompaniment to grilled meat. You can prepare it before grilling the meat and serve it in little dishes, garnished with chopped herbs.

Tip:

You can also add a crushed clove of garlic according to taste or – if you like it spicy – finely chop a chilli and add it to the puree.

Rice with Various Side Dishes

Plov

Serves 4 / 40 minutes

500 g Basmati rice
Salt
½ tsp ground turmeric or a few threads of saffron
40 g clarified butter

Put the turmeric or threads of saffron in a glass: pour on half a glass of hot water and leave to infuse. Melt the clarified butter in a pan over a medium heat.

Bring 1 ½ - 2 litres salted water to the boil in a large saucepan. Half-cook the rice in the salted water for approx. 8 minutes; be sure not to overcook the rice. Drain the rice. Using a pan with a thick base (a non-stick pan or a rice cooker is best), first of all put 3-4 tbsp rice in the pan, then add 1 tbsp turmeric or saffron water and 1 tbsp melted butter. Continue until the rice and the other ingredients have been used up. Cover the pan and leave to cook slowly for at least 30 minutes.

Tip: So that the rice at the bottom of the pan does not get hard or burn, you can put 1–2 peeled potatoes cut into thin slices or a thin slice of flatbread (yucha-lavasch, see p. ##) under the rice.

Side dishes to serve with rice

Lamb with Dried Fruit and Onions

Ash Gara

Serves 4 / 1 ½ hours

800 g lamb for braising (alternatively: beef or veal)
2 large onions
50 g clarified butter
100 g chestnuts, ready to cook
100 g dried soft apricots
100 g raisins
Salt
Freshly ground black pepper
1 pinch ground caraway seeds

Trim the meat, using a sharp knife to remove any fat and connective tissue, and cut into largish pieces. Gently simmer in a large pan of salted water over medium heat for approx. 20 minutes. Remove from the pan; strain and reserve the stock.

Peel the onions, halve them and cut into very fine strips lengthways. Melt the clarified butter in a frying pan and fry the onions until golden brown.

Return the meat to the saucepan and cover with the fried onions, chestnuts, soft apricots, and raisins. Season with salt, pepper, and caraway seeds, add the stock, cover and braise for 50–60 minutes until the meat virtually disintegrates.

The rice can be sprinkled with a little cinnamon before serving.

Meat Stew in Walnut and Pomegranate Sauce

Fesenjan

Serves 4 / 60 minutes

800 g lamb for braising (alternatively: beef or veal)
2 large onions
50 g clarified butter
100 g finely chopped walnuts
4 tbsp pomegranate syrup
Juice of 1 lemon
Salt
Freshly ground black pepper

Trim the meat and cut into pieces approx. 3 x 3 cm using a sharp knife. Gently simmer in a large pan of salted water over medium heat for approx. 20 minutes. Remove from the pan and keep warm; strain and reserve the stock.

Peel the onions and chop finely. Melt the clarified butter in a pan and fry the onions until golden brown. Add the meat and fry both together for 10–15 minutes. Gradually add the walnuts, pomegranate juice, lemon juice, salt, pepper, and ½ cup stock and continue to cook gently over a low heat until the meat is tender. Stir from time to time to prevent the meat sticking to the pan; add extra stock if necessary. The dish should not be dry but should have a thick consistency and a dark colour.

The rice can be sprinkled with a little cinnamon before serving.

Tip: Fisindschan can also be prepared using minced meat. In this case, chop an onion very finely and mix with the minced meat; season with salt and pepper and form small meatballs; then continue as described above.

Fried Meat with Herbs

Sabzi Ghormeh

Serves 4 / 50 minutes

800 g lamb for braising (alternatively: beef or veal)
1 large onion
50 g clarified butter
4 bouquet each of parsley, coriander, dill, sorrel
200 g spinach
1 leek
Salt
Freshly ground black pepper
Juice of 1 lemon

Trim the meat, using a sharp knife to remove fat and connective tissue, and cut into pieces weighing approx. 30 g. Gently simmer in a large pan of salted water over medium heat for approx. 20 minutes. Remove from the pan; strain and reserve the stock.

Peel the onions and chop finely. Melt the clarified butter in a pan and briefly fry the onions together with the meat, then add some of the stock. Wash the herbs and shake them dry; pluck the leaves from the stalks and chop them coarsely. Wash and clean the spinach and the leek, and chop coarsely. Gradually add the chopped herbs, the spinach, and the leek to the fried meat. Stir occasionally to prevent burning and add more stock as required. Make sure the consistency does not become too thick. Season with salt and pepper and add lemon juice to taste. Sabzi Ghormeh should have a slightly acid taste.

Plov for a Festive Occasion

Shah-Plow

Steps and recipe photo on double page 112/113

Serves 6 / 1 ½ hours

For the meat:
600 g lamb without fat and bones
(alternatively: beef or veal)
200 g clarified butter
3 medium-sized onions
100 g chestnuts, ready to cook
100 g dried soft apricots
150 g stoned dates
Juice of ½ lemon
Salt
Freshly ground black pepper

For the rice:
600 g Basmati rice
½ tsp ground turmeric or a few threads of saffron
40 g clarified butter

For the dough:
200 g flour
30 g butter
1 egg
1 tbsp cream
1 pinch salt

Cut the meat into cubes measuring approx. 2 cm. Melt 100 g clarified butter in a large frying pan and brown the meat over a high heat. Remove and put on one side. Peel the onions, halve them and cut into very fine strips lengthways. Fry the onions until golden brown in the remaining clarified butter in the frying pan in which the meat was browned. Add the meat, the chestnuts, the dried fruits, and the lemon juice successively to the onions. Season with salt and pepper, continue to fry briefly and then remove from the stove.

For the pastry dough, knead together the flour, butter, egg, cream, and salt to produce a firm dough. Roll the dough out thinly on a floured work surface and then use it to line a greased pan, allowing the surplus dough to overlap and hang down the sides.

For the rice, put the turmeric or threads of saffron in a glass: pour on half a glass of hot water and leave to infuse. Pre-heat the oven to 180° C / 350° F (upper and lower heat).

Melt the clarified butter in a pan over a medium heat.

Bring 1 ½ - 2 litres salted water to the boil in a large saucepan. Half-cook the rice in the salted water for approx. 8 minutes and drain. Fill alternately the rice, 1 tbsp saffron or turmeric water, melted butter, the meat mixture and then more rice, 1 tbsp saffron or turmeric water and 1 tbsp melted butter into the pan lined with dough. Add more seasoning if required. Cover the rice mixture with the overlapping dough, put on the lid and bake for approx. 40 minutes in the pre-heated oven at 180° C / 350° F(upper and lower heat).

When cooked, unmould the plow onto a large, flat serving dish and cut off the lid using a sharp knife (see photos p.112). Or cut it into slices like a cake and separate the slices carefully.

Serve the rice with the crisp dough.

Tip:

Instead of making the pastry you can use ready-made puff pastry or yufka dough. When lining the pan, brush each sheet of pastry with butter.

Braised Chicken with Potatoes

Toyug bozartmasi

Serves 4 / 60 minutes

1 oven-ready chicken
8 medium-sized waxy potatoes
6 large beef tomatoes
3 large onions
4 tbsp clarified butter or vegetable oil
Salt
Freshly ground black pepper
4 tbsp fresh chopped herbs
(flat-leaf parsley, mint, dill, coriander)

Cut the chicken into pieces and simmer over moderate heat for approx. 20 minutes until half-tender; remove and strain off the stock.

In the meantime, peel the potatoes and cut into quarters. Cut the tomatoes crosswise with a sharp knife, scald with boiling water, remove the skin and cut the flesh into small pieces. Peel and halve the onions and cut into fine slices.

Heat the clarified butter in a large pan, add the chicken pieces and fry for a few minutes. Add the onions and tomato pieces and fry for a further ten minutes. Finally add the quartered potatoes. Season with salt and pepper, cover and braise over a low heat until the potatoes are tender. Stir carefully from time to time.

Finely chop the herbs and sprinkle over the dish before serving.

Tip:

This hearty dish is a complete meal and also tastes excellent if re-heated the following day.

Mixed Grilled Meat Platter

Lyula, Tike and Toyug Kebab

Serves 4 / 20–30 minutes

Lyula Kebab:
400 g minced meat (minced lamb, beef, or veal)
1 large onion
Salt
Freshly ground black pepper

Tike Kebab:
4 lamb chops (alternatively: fillet of lamb, beef, or veal)
1 sprig thyme
1 medium onion

Toyug Kebab:
4 small chicken legs
8 chicken wings
1 medium onion
1 sprig thyme

And also:
Freshly chopped herbs according to taste
9 thin flatbreads
Lemon slices
Onion rings
Pomegranate syrup
Sumach
Pickled vegetables

For Lyula Kebab

Peel and chop the large onion very finely, either with a food chopper or a knife. Add the minced meat and mix well, either in the food chopper or with your hands. Season the meat with salt and pepper. Form the meat into balls, cover, and chill in the refrigerator for approx. 30 minutes.

For Tike Kebab

Season the lamp chops (or fillets of meat) with salt and pepper. Wash the thyme and shake dry. Pluck the thyme leaves off the twig. Peel the onion and cut into thin rings. Add the thyme leaves and onion rings to the meat and mix well. Cover and leave to marinate for 30 minutes.

For Toyug Kebab

Season the chicken with salt and pepper. Prepare as described for Tike Kebab above. Also leave the chicken to marinate for 30 minutes.

Pre-heat the grill in the oven to maximum heat or prepare the charcoal grill. Form the minced meat into long, thin meat patties; knock the thyme leaves and onion rings off the pieces of meat and chicken. Lay everything in the oven or on the grill and grill on either side for approx. 10–15 minutes.

Lay a flatbread on a large, flat serving dish. Arrange the grilled meat on top and decorate with fresh herbs and slices of lemon or onion rings. Serve the pomegranate syrup, sumach, and pickled vegetables separately. A good accompaniment would be a fresh tomato and cucumber salad with herbs.

Tip:

In Azerbaijan, kebab dishes are frequently served with stewed cornel cherries. Since they are hardly available here you can substitute chutneys with a sharp taste.

Home-made Pasta with Fried Minced Meat and Onions

Giyme Chingal

Serves 4 / 30 minutes

For the meat:
9 medium-sized onions
3 tbsp clarified butter
600 g minced meat (minced lamb, veal, or beef)
Salt
Freshly ground black pepper

For the pasta dough:
400 g flour
1 egg
Salt

And also:
500 g plain yoghurt
3–4 cloves garlic

For the meat, peel and finely dice 3 onions. Heat 2 tbsp clarified butter in a frying pan and sear the onions and the minced meat over a high heat. Season with salt and pepper.

Peel and halve the remaining onions and cut into fine slices, or shred them before frying in a second frying pan until golden brown.

To make the pasta, knead together the flour, egg, salt, and a little lukewarm water to make a smooth dough. Form the dough into 4 balls, cover and leave to rest for a while.

Press the garlic through the garlic press and mix with the yoghurt.

Roll the balls of dough out thinly, using a rolling pin or a pasta machine. Cut into diamond shapes (5 x 5 cm) and lay on a tea towel sprinkled with flour. Sprinkle some more flour on the pieces of dough.

Bring a large pan of water with a cooking insert to the boil and add ½ tsp salt. Add a few pasta sheets at a time and cook, stirring carefully to prevent their sticking. The pasta sheets are cooked once they rise to the surface.

Remove the pasta from the pan using a slotted spoon; arrange on 4 deep plates. Spoon the meat and the fried onions on the pasta; serve the garlic and yoghurt sauce separately.

Tip:

The side dishes served to accompany this pasta dish vary according to region. You can serve the dish with pomegranate syrup or sprinkle pomegranate seeds on the meat.

Stir-fried Meat and Vegetables

Sadj-Ichi

Before gas and electric stoves were invented, meals were cooked in the sadsch. This traditional cast-iron cooking utensil was widely found especially in the villages of western Azerbaijan. It can be compared with a large wok. When placed on the fire with the curved surface upwards it can be used to bake bread, lavash, and gutab; if turned the other way round it can be used for cooking. In former times the peasants would take the sadsch with them when they led their animals up onto the summer pastures. Archaeological excavations in some regions of what is now Azerbaijan have revealed a sadsch made of clay which is thought to date back to the fourth century BC. From the seventeenth century people started to produce sadsch made of cast iron.

For a number of years now a miniature variant of the sadsch has acquired a firm place in modern kitchens. Dishes prepared in the sadsch are called "Sadj-ichi". Chicken, lamb, and beef or fish are combined with vegetables according to taste.

To recreate this dish at home you can use a wok or a deep cast-iron frying pan.

Serves 4 / 40 minutes

800–900 g lamb (alternatively: chicken legs or fillet of beef)
4 plum tomatoes
4 green pointed peppers
4 medium-sized aubergines
Salt
4 medium-sized onions
4 medium-sized potatoes
Clarified butter
Freshly ground black pepper

Trim the meat, using a sharp knife to remove fat and connective tissue and cut into portions. Wash the vegetables. Leave the tomatoes and the pointed peppers whole. Peel the aubergines with the vegetable peeler, remove the stalk with a knife, and cut into slices lengthways. Sprinkle with salt and leave to stand for 30 minutes. Then rinse away the salt under running water and pat the aubergine slices dry with kitchen paper. Peel and halve the onions and cut into thin slices. Cut the potatoes into thin slices.

Heat the clarified butter in a wok or frying pan over a high heat and brown the meat. Season with salt and pepper and remove. Add the sliced potatoes, aubergines, and onions as well as the peppers and tomatoes. Season with salt and pepper and remove. Finally return the meat to the wok and cover with the potato and vegetable mixture, cover with a lid and allow to cook gently for 15–20 minutes on the stove or in the pre-heated oven at 150-180°C.

This dish is served hot directly from the wok.

Serve it with fresh flatbread. The Sadj-ichi can be garnished with fresh chopped herbs before serving.

Fried Lamb's Liver

Gara jiyer govurmasi

Serves 4 / 30 minutes

400–500 g fresh lamb's liver
3 medium-sized onions
400–500 g waxy potatoes
4–5 tbsp clarified butter or vegetable oil
Salt
Freshly ground black pepper

And also:
Fresh chopped herbs (mint, parsley, dill, coriander)
Fresh flatbread

Wash the lamb's liver and pat dry with a paper towel. Trim using a sharp knife to remove any sinews and fat, then cut into small pieces. Spread out on a paper towel to remove any surplus moisture.

Peel the onions and dice finely. Peel and dice the potatoes. Heat the clarified butter or vegetable oil in a large frying pan. Add first the onions and then the liver; sear briefly over a high heat. Add the diced potatoes, lower the heat, cover and cook for about 20 minutes until the potatoes are tender, stirring frequently. When cooked, season with salt and pepper.

Sprinkle the lamb's liver with the fresh herbs and serve hot, accompanied by crisp white bread or thin flatbread.

The sturgeon, a very fine culinary speciality, is indigenous to the Caspian Sea, the world's largest inland lake. It is popular not only for its delicious red flesh, but also for its sturgeon roe or caviar.

Grilled Fillet of Sturgeon

Nere balighi kababi

Serves 4 / 30 minutes

4 tbsp crème fraîche
4 tbsp tomato puree
2 tbsp cooking oil
Salt
Freshly ground black pepper
4 sturgeon fillets (alternatively: swordfish fillets)

And also:
Fresh herbs (e.g. coriander, flat-leaf parsley, basil, dill)
Slices of lemon
Preserved olives
Fresh flatbread

Pre-heat the oven on the grill setting to maximum heat. Stir together the crème fraîche, tomato puree, oil, salt, and pepper to make a marinade. Brush the fish fillets with it and leave to marinate for 20 minutes. Lay the fish fillets on a baking tray and grill for 15-20 minutes until tender.

Garnish the fish fillets with herbs, lemon slices, and olives, and serve with fresh flatbread.

Instead of fresh vegetables, the fish can also be served with a fresh salad or marinated vegetables. This dish tastes particularly good with pomegranate syrup or sumach.

Tip:

The fish fillets can also be cooked over a charcoal grill.

Fillet of Sturgeon on Vegetables

Bughlama

Serves 4 / 30 minutes

2 medium-sized onions
2 red bell peppers
4 large tomatoes
4 sturgeon fillets, cleaned and ready to cook
(alternatively: swordfish fillets)
Salt
Freshly ground black pepper
1 bouquet each flat-leaf parsley, coriander, dill
3 spring onions
4 tbsp cooking oil
½ cup water
50 g dried cranberries or morello cherries

Peel and halve the onions and cut into fine slices.

Wash and halve the bell peppers, remove the stalks and seeds, and cut into strips. Cut the tomatoes crosswise with a sharp knife, scald with boiling water, remove the skin and cut the flesh into eight pieces.

Put the vegetables in layers in a pan, lay the fish fillets on the vegetables, and season with salt and pepper.

Pre-heat the oven to 150° C / 300° F (upper and lower heat). Wash the herbs and shake dry; reserve a few sprigs for garnishing and chop the rest finely. Slice the spring onions finely. Sprinkle over the fish together with the herbs; pour on the oil and water. Sprinkle the dried cranberries or morello cherries on top of the herbs. Cover and cook on the hob for 15 minutes. Put in the pre-heated oven and bake for a further 30 minutes until cooked.

Arrange the fish fillets and vegetables on plates, garnish with the fresh herbs, and serve with fresh bread or steamed rice.

The kutum (*omul*), a native species of fish found in the Caspian Sea, is used for this traditional Azerbaijani dish. Since this species is not available in Western Europe, we recommend using other species of white fish such as bream or roach as a substitute.

Stuffed Fish

Kutum-Levengi

Serves 4 / 50 minutes

For the filling:
1 large onion
2 tbsp clarified butter
100 g raisins
100 g dried cherries or cranberries
100 g chopped walnuts
5 tbsp pomegranate syrup (*narscharab*)
Salt
Freshly ground black pepper

Fish:
4 bream or roach, cleaned and ready to cook

And also:
1 bouquet fresh dill
2 lemons
Toothpicks

For the filling, peel and chop the onions finely. Melt the clarified butter in a frying pan and lightly fry the onions until golden brown. Stirring continuously, add in succession the raisins, cherries or cranberries, walnuts, and 4 tbsp pomegranate syrup. Deglaze with 150 ml water and season with salt and pepper. Bring briefly back to the boil and then remove from the hob.

Rinse the cleaned fish thoroughly under running cold water and pat dry. Rub inside and out with salt, spoon in the filling, and close with the toothpicks. Baste with the remaining pomegranate syrup.

Pre-heat the oven to 180-190° C / 350-375° F (upper and lower heating elements). Line a baking tray with baking paper and place the fish with the back upwards on the tray. Bake in the oven for approx. 40 minutes.

Garnish the fish with lemon slices and dill to serve. Serve with additional pomegranate syrup at wish. This fish dish tastes excellent when served with fresh bread or rice.

Sherbet

Sherbet, in all its variations, is the most popular drink in Azerbaijan, after tea.

It is prepared from fresh fruits such as lemons, apricots, mirabelles, pomegranates, or any sort of berry. And then there are variants made with saffron, mint, rose petals, or dried herbs. The basic recipe involves making a syrup using sugar and water and then pouring the syrup over the fruits or leaves while it is still hot. In order to make a sherbet using basil, mint, or coriander seeds, you should first cook the seeds in water and then dissolve the sugar in the hot water. You can also season the sherbet with a shot of rose water. The sherbet should then be chilled in the fridge for about 4 hours and allowed to infuse. It is very refreshing when served with ice on a hot day.

Pomegranate Sherbet

120 ml water
30 g sugar
40 ml pomegranate juice from 2 large pomegranates
Ice cubes

Bring the water to the boil in a pan and dissolve the sugar completely. Allow the syrup to cool down to room temperature. Extract the juice from the pomegranates and mix the juice with the syrup. Cover and infuse by chilling in the fridge for at least 4 hours. Serve with ice cubes and pomegranate seeds.

The variety of fruits grown in Azerbaijan is quite
remarkable – and so are all the specialities produced
from those fruits.
Fresh walnuts are preserved in a very subtle way; rose
petals are made into a preserve; and even melon skins
are cooked with sugar. These delicious preserves are
part of any festive meal, or they are served with tea or
simply eaten at any time.

Walnut Preserve

Goz murebbesi

50 unripe green walnuts
1 kg sugar
10 cloves
Juice of 1 lemon
500 g pure lime

Shell the walnuts and cover with cold water. Soak for 3 days,
changing the water 2–3 times every day. Then lay the walnuts
in lime water*. Soak in lime water for 3 days, changing the water
4–5 times every day. Remove the walnuts, and using a sharp knife,
pierce the surface down to the kernel of the nut. Then cover the
walnuts with fresh, cold water once more. Soak for 3 days, changing the water 2–3 times every day. Remove the walnuts. Bring
plenty of water to the boil in a large pan; add the walnuts and
simmer for approx. 20 minutes. Remove and drain well.

Bring the sugar to the boil in a pan with 200 ml water. Add the
walnuts and simmer over a low heat for a few minutes. Stir from
time to time. Remove from the stove and leave the nuts to cool
for 4–5 hours. Bring the nuts to the boil and simmer for a few
minutes again 2–3 times more, leaving them each time to cool
down again in between. The last time you do this, add the cloves
and lemon juice. Pour the preserve into sterile preserving jars,
close with an airtight seal and leave to infuse for at least 20 days.

*To make the lime water, slake 500 g pure lime in 3 litres water,
leave to stand for 3–4 hours and then drain the clear water above
the lime through a sieve and use as above.

Rose Petal Preserve

Gizigul murebbesi

250 g untreated fragrant rose petals
1250 g sugar
2 tsp lemon juice

Separate the rose petals from the flower heads. Cut off the white ends using a pair of scissors. Mix the coloured parts of the petals with 750 g sugar, cover and leave to stand for 2 days. Put the white parts of the petals in a bowl, pour over 250 ml warm water, cover with a damp cloth, and leave to stand for 1 day. Pour off and save the water. Dissolve the remaining sugar in this rose water. After 2 days knead the sugared rose petals. Stir the syrup prepared using the white parts of the petals and strain through a sieve into the pan with the sugared rose petals. Bring to the boil over a low heat. Use a slotted spoon to remove any scum that rises to the top during cooking. Add the lemon juice. Once the syrup starts to thicken, remove it from the hob. Let the jam cool down, pour it into preserving jars and seal with an airtight lid.

Crab Apple Preserve (Paradise Apples)

Jennet almasi murebbesi

500 g crab apples
600 g sugar

Wash the crab apples, remove the stalk, and pierce several times with a fork. Bring 200 ml water to the boil in a large pan and add the apples. Reduce the heat, blanch for approx. 3 minutes and remove. Dissolve the sugar in the water and return to the stove. As soon as the syrup begins to boil, add the blanched apples and simmer for approx. 5 minutes over a low heat. Remove any scum which forms. Remove the preserve from the heat, leave to cool for 6–8 hours, and then boil again for another approx. 7–10 minutes. Pour into sterile preserving jars whilst still hot and seal with an airtight lid.

White Cherry Preserve

Ag gilas murebbesi

500 g pitted white cherries
600 g sugar
2 tsp lemon juice
Vanilla or cardamom

Put the cherries in a large pan, cover with sugar, and leave to marinate for 3–5 hours, or if possible overnight. Add 200 ml water and cook for 6–8 minutes over a low heat, remove from the stove, and leave to stand for 5–6 hours. Repeat this procedure a total of three times. During the last cooking time, add the lemon juice and vanilla or cardamom to taste. Pour into sterile preserving jars whilst still hot and seal with an airtight lid.

Cornel Cherry Preserve

Zogal murebbesi

500 g cornel cherries
600 g sugar
200 ml water

Use the same method as for the white cherry preserve. Cornel cherry preserve is cooked in two stages with a resting period of 5–8 hours.

Water Melon Rind Preserve

Garpiz murebbesi

500 g melon rind
600 g sugar
Vanilla
2 tsp lemon juice

For this preserve, use water melons with a thick skin. Remove the green outer rind in a generous layer. Cut the white skin into cubes and put in a pan. Cover with the sugar and leave to marinate over night. Cook in 3 stages with an 8-hour pause in between. During the last cooking time, add the vanilla and lemon juice. Pour into sterile preserving jars whilst still hot and seal with an airtight lid.

Sweet Flaky Pastry Squares

Pakhlavah

Quantities for 1 baking tray / 70 minutes

For the pastry:
approx. 20 g fresh yeast
approx. 100 ml lukewarm milk
500 g flour
1 pinch salt
2 egg yolks
150 g sour cream
100 g melted butter
1 generous pinch ground turmeric
2 packets vanilla sugar
½ tsp ground cardamom

For the filling:
500 g ground nuts (e.g. hazelnuts)
500 g sugar
2 packets vanilla sugar
½ tsp ground cardamom

And also:
approx. 500 g butter
2 egg yolks
2 tbsp milk
1 generous pinch ground turmeric
approx. 200 g whole nuts (the same sort as the filling)
250–300 g honey
Flour for the work surface
A deep, round baking tin (approx. 30 cm Ø;
a cake tin is not suitable)
12 baking cases

To make the pastry dough, crumble the yeast into the milk; put the flour, salt, egg yolks, and remaining ingredients for the dough in a large mixing bowl. Use your hands to knead to form a smooth dough. The dough should be soft but dry. If it seems too sticky, sprinkle a little flour on the dough and knead again. Cover the dough and leave to rise in a warm place (e.g. in the oven at 70° C / 160° F) for 20 minutes.

In the meantime, prepare the filling. Mix the ground nuts thoroughly with the other ingredients and put to one side.

Grease the baking tin with a little butter. Melt the remaining butter in a pan over a medium heat. Form the dough into 10–12 balls. On a floured work surface, roll out the first ball of dough using a rolling pin until it is somewhat larger than the diameter of the baking tin. Lay the dough in the tin, pull the sides up, press down firmly, and brush the surface with butter. Roll out the second ball of dough to the size of the base of the baking tin and lay it on the first layer. Brush again with butter and sprinkle 2–3 heaped tbsp of the nut filling on top. Continue in this manner until you reach the last but one ball of dough. Brush it with butter but do not add any more filling. Then add the final layer of dough but do not brush with butter. Press the pastry edges firmly against the pastry lid so that the last layer does not

spread out during cooking. Using the palm of your hand, gently press the surface of the pastry downwards so that all the layers of pastry are joined together.

Mix together 2 egg yolks, the milk, and the ground turmeric. Cut the baklava into diamond shapes approx. 10 x 4 cm using a sharp knife. Carefully brush the portions of baklava with the egg mixture and press a nut into the centre of each diamond shape.

Pre-heat the oven to 200° C / 400° F (upper and lower heat). Pre-bake (or rather, dry out) the baklava for approx. 15 min. Remove the form from the oven, pour the rest of the butter over the surface, use the sharp knife again to mark out the diamond shapes and return the baklava to the oven. Bake for about another 30 minutes until the surface is golden yellow.

In the meantime, dissolve the honey in 200 ml water in a saucepan and then cook over a medium heat until a syrup is formed. Take the baklava out of the oven, pour over the warm syrup and leave to cool for approx. 10 minutes. Use a knife to separate the diamonds and remove from the tin whilst they are still warm. Set each diamond shape in a paper case and store in an airtight tin in a cool, dry place.

Tip:

If you are unaccustomed to making pastry and are short of time, you can also make baklava with the ready-to-use yufka, filo, or flaky pastry which can be purchased in the shops. The method remains the same.

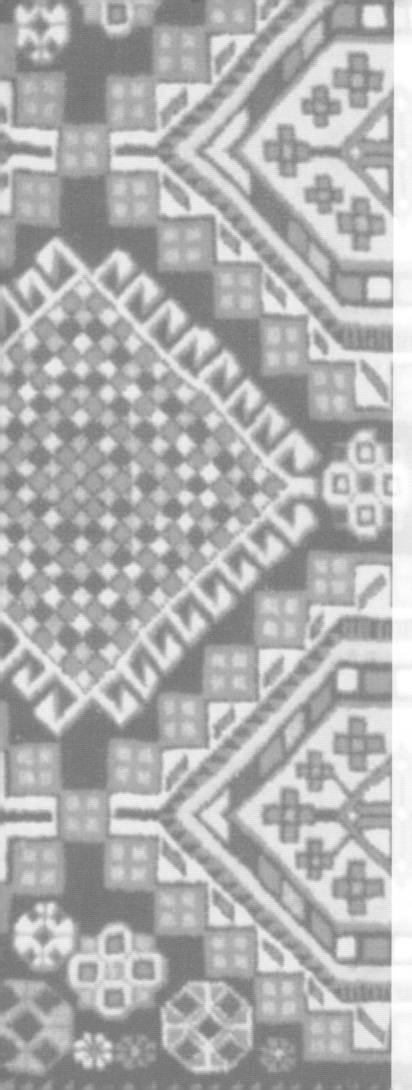

Sweet Pastry Crescents with Nut Filling

Shekerbura

For the pastry:
80 ml milk
10 g fresh baker's yeast
2 egg yolks
150 g sour cream
80–100 g melted butter
1 generous pinch ground turmeric
Salt
1 packet vanilla sugar
1/s tsp ground cardamom
500 g flour

For the filling:
500 g shelled and roasted almonds or other nuts according to taste
(alternatively: used ready-ground nuts)
500 g sugar
1 packet vanilla sugar
1 tsp ground cardamom

For the pastry, gently warm the milk and crumble the yeast into it to dissolve. Use a spoon to mix together all the other ingredients for the pastry. Then gradually stir in the milk and yeast, and knead the dough until it is smooth. The dough should be smooth but relatively firm. Form the dough into approx. 25–30 small balls (approx. 20–30 g each), arrange them on a plate and cover with cling film. Leave the dough to rest in a cool place.

For the filling, grind the nuts finely or coarsely according to taste and mix with the other ingredients.

Pre-heat the oven to 180° C / 360° F (upper/lower heat). Roll out each ball of dough approx. 2 cm thick (smaller than a saucer), put 1 heaped tbsp of the filling in the middle of the circle and fold into a crescent shape. Pinch the edges firmly with thumb and forefinger, and then pull gently and twist to form a decorative edging (you could also use a ravioli maker for this). Then decorate the surface with special tongs (or you can use tweezers) in order to create a pine-cone pattern.

Place the crescent-shaped pastries – *shekerburas* – on a baking tray lined with baking paper and bake in the pre-heated oven at 180° C / 360° F for approx. 15–20 minutes. When the underside is fairly brown, remove the *shekerburas*. The surface should not be allowed to brown.

Rolls with Nut Filling

Ordubad durmesi

120 g butter
200 g sour cream
400 g flour
1 pinch salt
220 g walnuts
180 g sugar
40 g honey
2 tsp ground cinnamon
1 egg yolk

Beat the softened butter with a hand whisk until white and fluffy; gradually add the sour cream. Then add the flour and salt, and knead to form a dough. Divide the dough into three equal-sized pieces and form each into a ball. Cover the balls of dough and leave to rest.

Roast the walnuts in a non-stick pan without the addition of fat, leave to cool and grind finely using the chopper; alternatively, you can also chop the nuts very finely using a sharp knife. Add the honey and cinnamon, and mix thoroughly.

Pre-heat the oven to 190–200° C / 375–395° F (upper and lower heat). Line a baking tray with baking paper.

Roll out the dough on a floured surface until it is 3-4 mm thick. Spread one third of the walnut filling evenly across the dough. Roll the pastry up into a long roll, sealing the ends carefully. Repeat the process with the other balls of dough. Finally brush the rolls with egg yolk and bake for 30–35 minutes until golden brown.

Leave the rolls to cool before cutting them into slices with a sharp knife and serving.

Tip:

The dough can also be prepared with baking powder or yeast.

LIST OF PHOTOS

RUSSIAN FEDE

TBILISI

Kura

G E O R G I A

Balakan
Zagatala
Aliabad
Qakh
Shaki
Oghuz
Qab

Aghstafa
Qazakh
Tovuz
Kur
Dzegam
Samukh
Shamkir
GANJA
Geranboy
Gadabay
Goygol
NAFTALAN
Dashkasan
Goygol lake
Terter
Barda
Aghdara
MINGECHEVIR
Yevlakh
Aghdash
Goy
Lyaki
Ujar
Zardak

Iori
Qabyrri
Qanykh
Agrichay
Mingechevir reserv
Aljanchay
Kura

THE GREAT

THE SMALL CAUCASUS

GOYCHA LAKE

A R M E N I A

Kalbajar
İstisu
KHANKENDI
Lachin
Shusha
Aghdam
Khojali
Khojavand
Beylagan
Aghjabedi
Fuzuli
Hadrut
Horadiz
Qubadly
Jebrayil
Zangilan

Mil-Mugan reservoir

TURKEY
Heydarabad
Sharur
Araz
NAKHCHIVAN
Shahbuz
AZERBAIJAN REPUBLIC
Qivraq
"Araz" reservoir
NAKHCHIVAN
Babek
Julfa
Ordubad

I R A N

174

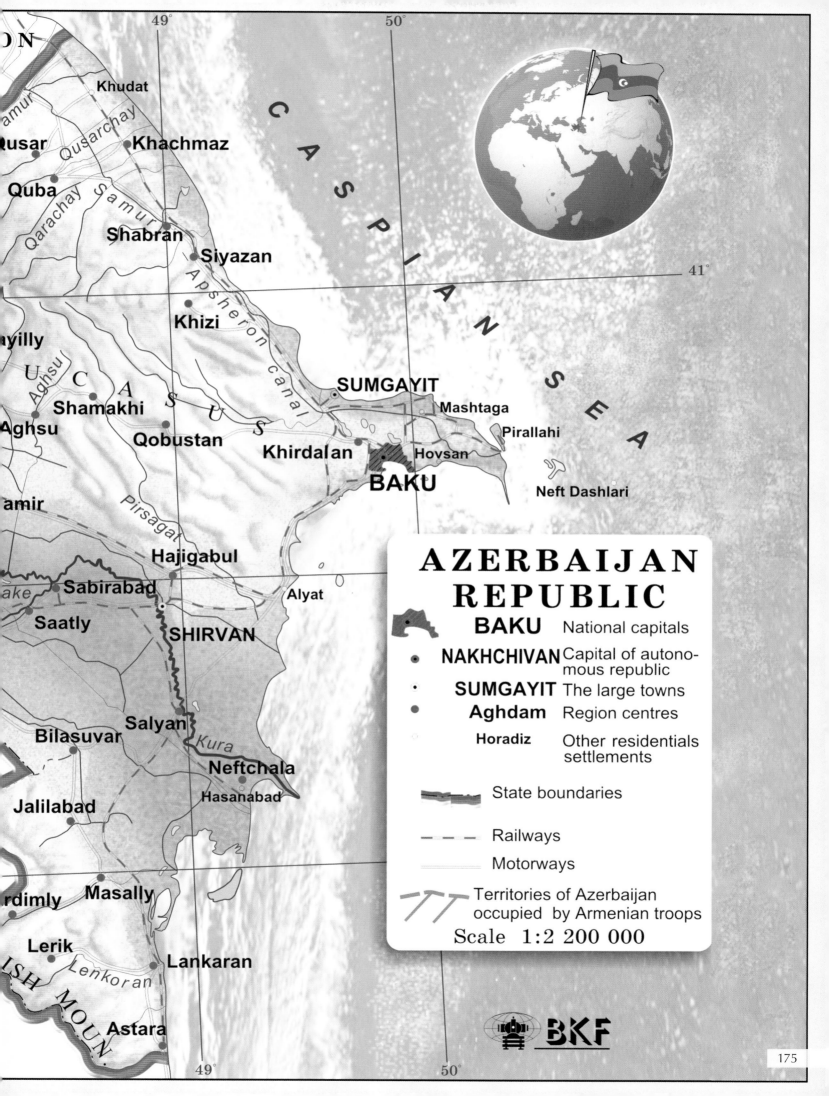

AZERBAIJAN REPUBLIC

BAKU National capitals

NAKHCHIVAN Capital of autono-
mous republic

SUMGAYIT The large towns

Aghdam Region centres

Horadiz Other residentials
settlements

State boundaries

Railways

Motorways

Territories of Azerbaijan
occupied by Armenian troops

Scale 1:2 200 000

BKF

ACKNOWLEDGEMENTS

It was a pleasure and an honour for me to be invited by the Heydar Aliyev Foundation and the State Committee for Diaspora in Baku.

I had the opportunity to get to know the country and its people as a photographer without having to find my own way around as regards research and travel throughout the country. The Minister, Nazim Ibrahimov, gave my ideas his personal attention. Thanks to the enthusiasm of the coordinator of this project, Arzu Tebrizli, special subjects and locations in Baku were placed at my disposal so that my wishes could be realised. The chairperson of the European Congress of Azerbaijanis, Samira Patzer-Ismailova, led the project with enthusiasm and thanks to her remarkable knowledge of the country guided me through the cities and landscapes of Azerbaijan. She showed me important cultural locations and sights, and her multilingual skills were used to best advantage. Eldar Isayev, our driver, drove us untiringly and with great patience from place to place. My thanks go also to the Gala Bazaar Restaurant and its talented and understanding chef de cuisine Ilham Mesimov and his hard-working assistant Torgul Rzazadek.

I should like to thank them all expressly for all their help!

1st edition 2016

Published by
Congress of European Azerbaijanis

Project Management and Editing
Arzu Tebrizli (Azerbaijan)
Samira Patzer - Ismailova (Germany)

Photographs and Cover Design
Barbara Lutterbeck

Publishing Coordination
Saskia Gehlen
Doris Hansmann

Graphic Design
Franziska Bucco

Design Advisor
Atelier Josef Schaller, Cologne

Typesetting and Photo Editing
Thorsten Laureck, Jörg Müller,
adhoc media GmbH

Text
Brunhild Seeler-Herzog
Barbara Lutterbeck

Recipes
Naiba Hantel
Barbara Lutterbeck

Translation (German-English)
Jane Michael, Munich

Published by
Wienand Verlag, Cologne
www.wienand-verlag.de

Bibliographic information published by the
Deutsche Nationalbibliothek
The Deutsche Nationalbibliothek lists this publication in the Deutsche Nationalbibliografie; detailed bibliographic data is available on the internet at http://dnb.d-nb.de.

ISBN 978-3-86832-316-0

This book was produced with the kind support of the Heydar Aliyev Foundation and the State Committee for Diaspora Affairs of the Republic of Azerbaijan.
We should like to thank the Congress of European Azerbaijanis for its assistance with organisational matters.